# Secr(
# West (

C000139524

*Exploring West Sussex with*
*eighteen tours and unusual places to visit.*

## Sandy Hernu

S.B. Publications

By the same author:
*Exploring Alfriston and the Cuckmere Valley*
*East Sussex Walks (Brighton, Eastbourne and Lewes area)*
*East Sussex Walks (In and around the rural villages)*
*East Sussex Walks (Exploring 1066 Country)*
*West Sussex Walks (Arundel, Steyning and Worthing area)*
*Secrets of East Sussex*

First published in 1997 by S.B. Publications
c/o 19 Grove Road, Seaford, East Sussex BN25 1TP

ISBN 1 85770 127 5

Typeset and printed by Island Press Ltd.
3 Cradle Hill Industrial Estate, Seaford, East Sussex BN25 3JE
Telephone: 01323 490222 UK

*Front Cover:*  Stopham Bridge, near Pulborough.
*Back Cover:*  Bosham.
*Title Page:*  Hollygate Cactus Gardens, Ashington.

*Front cover photography by Graham Thornton*

# CONTENTS

# INTRODUCTION

What can we do today? The answer to that question is, pick up a copy of the "Secrets of West Sussex", head for the car and the country and follow a self-guided tour. What could be simpler? There are no timetables or rules. You have been given the freedom of a gypsy wanderer to go hither and explore the hidden delights of the rich Sussex landscape.

Possibly this book could be described as a 'passport to ideas'. designed to introduce the many varied aspects of West Sussex in the form of easy-to-follow theme tours. Although each tour is planned to last about a day by car, they also offer great scope for any flexibility. For example, some of the slightly longer tours could be extended over two days; or you may prefer to select just two or three things to visit after a leisurely pub lunch. There is no reason why the cyclist should not scan these pages and borrow some ideas before free wheeling slowly through the country lanes. Perhaps the walker would like to take advantage of the trails indicated in a few of the tours, particularly those that explore the downstream passage of the three West Sussex rivers. If you prefer not to travel too far, there's a 'Pick and Mix' Geographical Index to choose from. Assuming you already have a road map, the numbers on the maps at the beginning of the tours, together with the information, should enable you to find each location fairly easily. And finally ...... I hope you find your travels through West Sussex are enjoyable, rewarding and fun.

*The Toll Bridge, Old Shoreham*

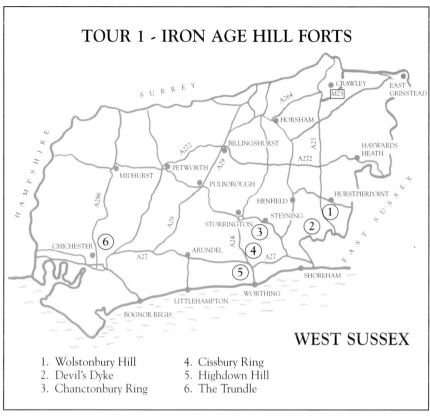

# TOUR 1 - IRON AGE HILL FORTS

**WEST SUSSEX**

1. Wolstonbury Hill
2. Devil's Dyke
3. Chanctonbury Ring
4. Cissbury Ring
5. Highdown Hill
6. The Trundle

*Chanctonbury Ring*

# TOUR 1 - IRON AGE HILL FORTS

*All you need for this tour is fine weather, a picnic and a modicum of imagination to bring to life those ghosts of the prehistoric past. Do you remember when it was all just a bit of dull old history at school? I'm pretty certain, after exploring one or two of these legendary hill forts, it won't be dull any longer; this, together with the ancient myths and fabulous views across the Sussex Weald to Beachy Head and the Isle of Wight are not to be missed. And if it rains ... then its wellies, Barbours and a thermos of hot coffee followed by a trip to the nearest pub to banish any hill top chill.*

*The Iron Age spans the years from 700 BC, when the Celtic groups started to infiltrate into Sussex, until the Roman Conquest of 43 AD. The remains of our predecessors' massive fortified hill top towns and villages still stretch across the downland, often giving a curious ribbed effect to the normally smooth green apex. With the onset of the Celtic groups becoming established in the south, so flint, the material that had been used for thousand of years for tools and weapons, was replaced by iron and the timber from the Wealden forests taken to feed the fires for iron smelting. Farming took on a different aspect in the Iron Age, as the growing of crops became preferable to the nomadic herding of the previous Bronze Age inhabitants. Evidence of the Celtic wooden houses and their domestic crafts, such as pottery and cloth making have been discovered within the hill forts. Smaller hamlets naturally existed throughout Sussex and whilst some have not yet been excavated, others will remain lost forever under the plough or development.*

## WOLSTONBURY HILL (1)

Owned by the National Trust, Wolstonbury is one of the older hill forts, thought to date from about 600 BC. The extremely pretty walk to get to the site of this Iron Age village is approximately two and a half miles, there and back. The bridlepath starts almost opposite the Jack and Jill pub on a minor road at Clayton, which is between Burgess Hill and Brighton on the A273. The easy route is signed but it could be advisable to consult the Ordnance Survey Pathfinder Map 1288, before setting off.

## DEVIL'S DYKE (2)

A name like Devil's Dyke indicates it was not simply evolution that caused this unusually clefted valley. It was, of course, the Devil himself, digging frantically away at the downland by night in order to let the sea flow freely across the Weald and drown all the churches, which he loathed. However, a wily old countrywoman foiled him by holding a candle behind a sieve to simulate a very early sunrise. He downed tools and fled for ever, leaving his work unfinished; the clods of earth he'd already tossed westwards supposedly formed Chanctonbury Ring!

Devil's Dyke can be reached by road from Brighton or Poynings. There are two Car Parks either side of the valley and by the northern one is the Devil's Dyke Hotel with the Iron Age hill fort just to the east. The scenery of the Dyke has attracted thousands of tourists for well over a hundred years, particularly during the late 19th century. To cater for all these visitors a railway was built during the 1880's

from Brighton to the Dyke and this was when the hotel began life as a humble refreshment bar. Simultaneously, a cable car was erected to cross the valley and a funicular to climb the north side of the Downs from Poynings. Today, crumbling walls of what could have been the ticket office and a few footings are all that remain.

## CHANCTONBURY RING (3)

There used to be a thick circular wood of beech trees set within the prehistoric earthworks on Chanctonbury. These were planted in 1760 by a Charles Goring who lived at the Elizabethan Wiston House at the foot of the Downs. Unfortunately, the number of trees has been diminished by the hurricane of 1987 and it all looks rather sparse.

At 783 feet, Chanctonbury is one of the highest points of the West Sussex downland, so apart from spectacular views, its Iron Age inhabitants would have had fair warning of any invaders. The same spot was favoured by the Romans, for as the Celts moved out of their hill fort, the Romans moved in and the remains of the square Romano-Celtic temple has yielded several important discoveries. Subsequently, the Saxons also chose this hill top to establish some sort of weird pagan shrine. Chanctonbury has its fair share of folklore too: supposedly the devil will appear, should you chose to run backwards round the ring. The tale about the ghost of a white-bearded man who once searched the summit for his buried gold, ended when some coins were dug up at Chancton Farm at the end of the 19th century and he was laid to rest. Nightfall on

Chanctonbury is reputed to be an evil time, for this is when the witches meet in the old Hill Fort!

Chanctonbury is indicated from the A283 west of Steyning. There is a bit of a trek to get to the Ring, but it's well worth it.

## CISSBURY RING (4)

Cissbury, owned by the National Trust, is one of the biggest and most exciting hill forts in Britain and thought to be the principal 'city' of the Iron Age communities in Sussex. The impressive ramparts encircle about sixty-five acres and the coastal panorama extends to the Isle of Wight. The construction of this fortified city began between 400 BC and 300 BC, the ramparts being in the form of a deep ditch and a bank with wooden palisades. It's uncertain how many timber buildings there were, or indeed how many people lived in Cissbury, but to keep such lengthy ramparts constantly manned would suggest a community of several thousand inhabitants.

However, the Iron Age dwellers were not the first residents of Cissbury. Around 3000 BC, Neolithic man had his flint mines on the western edge of the Ring and the bumps and undulations supply the visible evidence of Britain's earliest industry. Over two thousand flint mines have been located, some going down to a depth of forty feet or more. Briefly, Cissbury was occupied again in the latter part of the Roman occupation, when soldiers had to reinforce the old fort walls against repeated attacks from the Saxons.

To reach Cissbury Ring, take the turning to Findon from the A24, about four miles north of Worthing. Follow the road eastwards through the village and after passing Nepcote Green, continue uphill until reaching a small Car Park. The Ring will be on the right.

*The Hill Fort at Cissbury Ring*

## HIGHDOWN HILL (5)

Strategically positioned looking across the flat plain to the sea, this oddly cosy Iron Age fort is tucked well back on Highdown Hill. Today, the urban tentacles of the seaside resorts reach out intrusively, yet Highdown still manages to retain a sense of isolation. The formation of the ramparts began around 600 BC and whilst not as extensive as some of the other forts, Highdown is of significant archeological importance. Most of the artifacts found here are now in Worthing Museum. Prior to the Iron Age the site was occupied by a Bronze Age settlement, dating from 1000 BC and during the 19th century it was discovered to have been used as a Saxon cemetery from 450 AD.

Highdown Hill is owned by the National Trust and lies up a narrow lane off the A259 between Littlehampton and Worthing. There is a Car Park at the top of the hill and the ring is only a ten minute walk.

## THE TRUNDLE (6)

The glorious downland overlooking the Goodwood Estate and close to Goodwood Racecourse, goes by the odd name of 'The Trundle'; of Saxon origin it means 'circles'. This hill top bears the rather complicated earthworks of a strongly fortified enclosure with three circular banks. After Cissbury, it was the most important Iron Age fort in West Sussex. Its history is chequered to say the least; during Neolithic times it was a causewayed camp; Medieval times it played home to St. Roches Chapel and finally, a windmill stood there, faithfully grinding corn until the 18th century, when it caught fire.

The Trundle can be reached from the A286 at Singleton, five miles north of Chichester and the parking is reasonably close to the fort.

# TOUR 2 - ROMAN SUSSEX

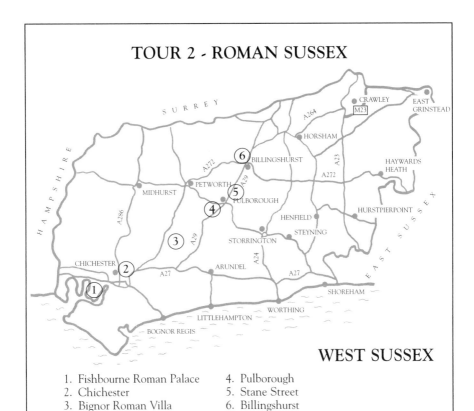

## WEST SUSSEX

1. Fishbourne Roman Palace
2. Chichester
3. Bignor Roman Villa
4. Pulborough
5. Stane Street
6. Billingshurst

*Mosaics at Bignor*

# TOUR 2 - ROMAN SUSSEX

History's jigsaw is complex and fascinating, yet in spite of ongoing research and evidence, it still leaves much to the imagination; this of course, arouses a hidden curiosity and the wish to learn more about our ancestors and the way they lived.

The Roman occupation of this country began in AD 43. After initial resistance a British leader, the crafty Cogidubnus, reckoned he'd be better off joining the Roman invaders and promptly set about trying to form an alliance with them. He succeeded and under their jurisdiction constituted local rule in Sussex and was given the status of a Roman Ambassador. He subsequently created his luxurious palace at Fishbourne and established Chichester as the capital town.

When they came to these shores the Romans brought with them a wealth, culture and technology, hitherto unknown here. They built cities, splendid basilicas, amphitheatres, bathhouses and rural villas: roads, harbours and trading centres were constructed. They farmed extensively, particularly in the lowland plains. The discovery of a number of domestic villas in West Sussex, indicates it being a favoured residential area. East Sussex and Kent were the industrial part, used mainly for iron smelting.

The stamp of Roman genius quickly spread across England from Fishbourne Palace in the south to Hadrians Wall in the north. Yet for all that genius, deep pockets of unrest grew throughout the country and there was an increasing threat of Saxon raids. By the middle of the third century the Romans were having to fortify their towns, re-establish and strengthen old hill forts and also build the massive new fort of Anderida at Pevensey in East Sussex. By 450 AD the Roman dynasty in Britain had collapsed; with their numbers dissipated, they were no match for the marauding Saxons and were consequently forced to withdraw their legions back to the Continent. Slowly their legacy of technology, like their great villas, crumbled into obscurity.

Today, where possible, those Roman remains have been preserved and give an excellent insight into what can only be described as a "sophisticated lifestyle". Do go and see the substantial north wing and formal gardens of the palace lived in by Cogidubnus at Fishbourne. Snippets of a Roman past crop up in Chichester, where one can almost feel that two thousand year old city lying beneath your feet, hushed and dreaming. Spend the afternoon at Bignor and see the relics of a Roman country villa filled with famous mosaics. Finally wend your way along Stane Street, once the main route to London.

## FISHBOURNE ROMAN PALACE (1)

The unprepossessing structure that covers the remains of this Roman palace, contradicts the ancient contents within. Fishbourne originally covered 5.6 acres; today most of those ruins lie buried forever under a housing estate and the A27, both built prior to proper archeological attention.

Sporadic discoveries of Roman materials have happened at Fishbourne since 1805. Yet it was not until 1960, when a worker chanced upon a pile of mosaics while digging, that the significance of the site was realized. The museum opened to the public in 1968.

*Plan of Fishbourne Roman Palace*

*Model of Roman Crane, Roman Palace, Fishbourne*

When the Romans landed in AD 43, Fishbourne was used as a harbour and military depot: there was a substantial granary and other buildings. It was not until around AD 75 that plans were made to build a sumptuous palace, laid out in the Italian fashion of a colonnaded entrance, a central courtyard and formal gardens, surrounded by a hundred rooms, mostly with mosaic floors.

The native King Cogidubnus was thought to be the creator and the occupier of this palatial residence: somewhat of a turncoat, his wealth and power grew substantially under Roman rule. By the end of the first century the palace was completed, but alterations and changes appeared to continue until AD 280, possibly because of rotting timbers or subsidence. By the end of the third century Fishbourne had been destroyed by a fire. The burnt out shell became the object of looting as people sifted through the remains for valuables and salvaged any building materials for their own use. With the Roman era declining, it was never rebuilt and as farming continued throughout the years, the site returned to arable land.

Fishbourne Roman Palace is situated just west of Chichester on the A259; owned by The Sussex Archeological Society, it's open daily, except in December, January and February, when it's Sundays only. There is an admission charge to visit.

## CHICHESTER (2)

Pinioned against the skyline, the spire of Chichester Cathedral rises above the fertile plain to look down on the medieval and Georgian architecture nudging those magnificent walls of The Holy Trinity. Yet beneath the beautiful City of Chichester lies another as, if not more, important than the one we see today.

The Roman town of Noviogamus (Chichester), grew to be an influential trading and administrative centre. It had roads connecting it with London, Southampton, Silchester and eastwards towards Angmering: it was easily accessible by the sea through Chichester Harbour. The town was fortified and had its own amphitheatre; identified in 1935 but sadly, not preserved.

Proper excavation of Novigamus is frustrating and almost impossible. The layout of the present city is very similar to that of its predecessor and therefore lies directly above the old Roman remains. Many of the buildings, such as the Basilica, are unlikely to ever be revealed. However the historical evidence and discoveries to date, which includes a Roman lead coffin, are chronicled and displayed in Chichester District Museum. This is housed in a converted corn mill in Little London and is open from Tuesdays to Saturdays. It's free, too.

Whilst in Chichester do have a look at the 18th century Council Chamber in North Street, not far from the Market Cross. Let into the wall under its arched facade is an inscribed Roman stone; it reads:-

"To Neptune and Minerva
      A Temple
For the well being of the Divine House
On the authority of Tiberius Claudius
Cogidubnus great King in Britain.
The Guild of Smiths and those therein
Gave it from their own resources...."

For further information on Chichester, see Tour 15 - "A Walk Round Chichester".

## BIGNOR ROMAN VILLA (3)

The Romans surely knew how to recognise a choice position. The siting of Bignor Villa is no exception. It's situated in a bowl of fertile land near an escarpment of wooded downland and close to Stane Street, the London to Chichester road. The villa, probably built by a rich merchant, was one of the largest in Britain and covered two hectares. The excellent quality of the soil naturally ensured rich farming and the indication of extensive barns imply large-scale agriculture. Bignor Villa was first discovered in 1811 by a farmer, George Tupper. He was ploughing his land when a piece of masonry struck the plough. Further excavations revealed the fine Ganymede mosaic. By 1814 foundations, other mosaics and artifacts had been unearthed, covered with a thatched building for protection and opened to the public as a museum. By 1815 over a thousand people had visited to see the evidence of a 'Roman home'. The villa is still owned by the Tupper family and it's open from March until the end of October. There is an admission charge. Bignor is situated about six miles north of Arundel and is signed from the A29 and the A285.

## PULBOROUGH (4)

Pulborough was a place of considerable note during Roman times, borne out by the local discoveries of villas, a temple, coins and artifacts. Its importance was due to Stane Street crossing the Arun at this point on the way to London. Evidence suggests it was fairly heavily guarded too.

Today, Pulborough is scattered, the heart divided by main roads and too much traffic. The pretty part with interesting buildings is sited on a hill around the church of St. Mary, which is approached by stone steps and a medieval lychgate.

## STANE STREET (5)

Built in the first century AD, Stane Street became the chief Roman road of Sussex, providing an important link between London and Chichester. It ran generally in the north east direction, close to Bignor Villa then via Hardham, Pulborough, Billingshurst, Alfoldean, Ockley and Dorking, entering London near Tower Bridge. At Hardham and Alfoldean there is evidence of old Posting Stations. These were positioned at intervals along most roads to provide food, water and a change of horse, thus ensuring a speedy and efficient delivery service.

If you feel like a short Roman ramble, consult the Pathfinder map 1287 and take one of the footpaths just south of Pulborough that passes the site of an old Roman Bath House; this is indicated on the map. Or, you could take the A29 north of Pulborough to Billingshurst. Here the road is long and straight and covers the identical track as that of the Roman Stane Street. You just need to imagine you're riding in a chariot, instead of a car!

## BILLINGSHURST (6)

An oversized village that supposedly acquired its name from the Roman engineer, Belinus, who built Stane Street and then went on to carve a great path through the dense Wealden forests so the route could reach London. Somewhere, the handsome Norman church has a few Roman bricks pinning a part of the hefty foundations. Inside is an unusual panelled wood ceiling with carved bosses. In later years, Billingshurst became an important coaching village and amongst the many timber framed properties is the 16th century 'Ye Old Six Bells', one of several old coaching inns that still serve pints today.

*The Minerva Stone, Chichester*

15

# TOUR 3 - NORMAN SUSSEX

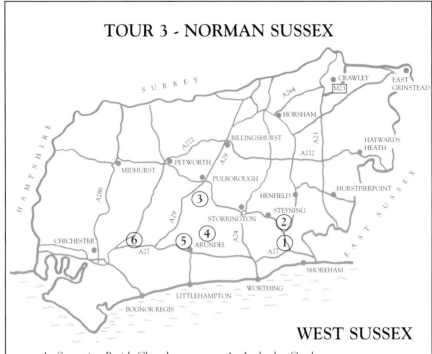

## WEST SUSSEX

1. Sompting Parish Church
2. Bramber Castle
3. St. Botolph's Church, Hardham
4. Amberley Castle
5. Arundel Castle
6. Boxgrove Priory

*Sompting Church*

# TOUR 3 - NORMAN SUSSEX

There are almost six hundred years between the departure of the Romans and the Norman Conquest of 1066. What happened to the legacy of the Roman civilization after the Saxon invasions of the 5th century, is a mystery. Probably in this rather obscure period one must assume constant in-fighting led to the gradual abandonment of towns and villas as the Saxons moved through Britain, dividing the country into small locally ruled kingdoms. They established the village settlement and these were inhabited not only by the Saxons from northern Germany, but the Angles from the borders of Germany and Denmark, plus the Jutes from Rhineland. However, from the 8th century onwards, this Anglo Saxon mix were constantly under attack from the Vikings. It was after such an attack that a wearied Saxon army led by Harold, fought the Norman army at the Battle of Hastings in 1066.

Enter William the Conqueror, whose victorious assault over King Harold eventually proved to be something of a political watershed. History now seems to become tangible and easier to charter; maybe the Domesday Survey of 1086 has something to do with it; or could it be the great Norman castles, visible today, fire the imagination to re-create the distant past without too much effort? Examples of their churches, still used by thousands, stretch throughout the county, occasionally retaining some distinctive Saxon features, known as the Saxon - Norman overlap period

Almost immediately after the Conquest, William divided Sussex into six administrative sections called 'Rapes'. These ran from the north to the south of the county and each had a castle, a river and a harbour. They were respectively: Hastings, Pevensey and Lewes in East Sussex: Bramber, Arundel and Chichester in West Sussex.

The Norman Tour, which is a fairly long one, follows the early days of their occupation and visits places, often previously occupied by Saxons, but rebuilt on a grander scale by William's henchmen after the Conquest. Possibly the masterpiece of Norman architecture is Chichester Cathedral, constructed when the Bishopric was moved from Selsey to Chichester around 1075. The Cathedral is not included on this route, but in Tour 15 - 'A Walk Around Chichester'.

## SOMPTING PARISH CHURCH, SOMPTING (1)

Sompting Church is one of those ancient pearls captured in a historical oyster. The unusual structure sits back against the lower slopes of downland, isolated from its former village by the busy A27 dual carriage way. The church still possesses a Saxon tower with four gables, a style known as a 'Rhenish Helm' or 'Rhineland Helmet' and whilst not uncommon in the Rhineland of Germany, it's the only remaining example in this country. The body of the church is mainly Norman and the charming interior contains both Norman and Saxon characteristics, including a 12th century font made of Sussex marble. Outside, the extensively terraced churchyard is beautifully kept and in spite of it's proximity to the coastal resort of Worthing, feels oddly continental and very peaceful.

To get to Bramber Castle from Sompting Church, follow the minor road northwards across an expanse of downland that can't have altered too much since 1066.

# BRAMBER CASTLE, BRAMBER (2)

Positioned by the A283 on a chalky hillock, Bramber Castle has a bird's eye view across the River Adur to Shoreham and the sea. After the Conquest the Rape of Bramber was bestowed on William de Braose and it was he who built the castle to guard the river and the Sussex coastline. The Adur was a good deal wider (and deeper) then and actually reached the foot of the castle walls. This enabled a flourishing port to become established and a small town grew up along the water's edge. Unfortunately, during the 12th century, the river began silting up and the port of Bramber could no longer operate; it was re-sited initially at Old Shoreham before moving yet again to New Shoreham.

The Castle remained in the de Braose family until 1326 and thereafter had several owners and a fairly uneventful history until the Civil War, when it was besieged by the Parliamentary Army. It is thought they left it in a ruinous state. In 1925 Bramber Castle was purchased by the National Trust and it's now in the care of English Heritage. Although the well preserved remains are few, apart from a notable wall of the Keep, it makes a delightful and interesting place to visit at any time. The curious truncated tower of the adjacent St. Nicholas Church is attributed to a castle wall falling on top of it.

# ST. BOTOLPH'S CHURCH, HARDHAM (3)

A pretty little whitewashed church sited close to Pulborough Brooks in the hamlet of Hardham, south of Pulborough on the A29. It's almost certain that St. Botolph's is of the pre-Conquest era and it does contain a number of the Saxo-Norman features. What is unique about this church are the interior two-tier wall paintings which date from about 1100 AD. They are thought to be amongst the most important in England and were first discovered in 1862, when their covering of plaster was chipped away in the chancel arch. The delicate task of exposing the rest of the paintings has been done in various stages over a number of years and it appears the upper tier is in a better of preservation than the lower. The frescoed subjects include; Adam and Eve, the Infancy and the Passion, the Labours of the Months and various other biblical scenes. An informative guide about the paintings can be obtained inside the church.

# AMBERLEY CASTLE (4)

Amberley is one of the loveliest Sussex villages, protected by the south westerly sweep of Amberley Castle's Curtain Wall. This rather forbidding facade was constructed about 1380 in order to protect Bishop Rede's overly lavish palace within from any raids. It proved to be unnecessary and today the crenellated frontage is incorporated with the Tudor Manor behind to make up an exclusive Country Hotel. The ruins of the Bishop's 12th century castle, or palace (which I paid a shilling to play in as a child) are now blended into the charming hotel gardens. If this was made a rather special lunch stop it would, of course, enable you to see the Castle in its entirety.

*Amberley Castle*

# ARUNDEL CASTLE (5)

In a beautiful hillside setting Arundel Castle guards the gap in the South Downs formed by the River Arun. It's turreted fairy tale image is mainly Gothic but its origins are pure Norman, evident by the 12th century Keep and 13th century Barbican, restored and combined with the body of the Castle.

The Earldom of Arundel was conferred by William on Roger de Montgomery soon after the Conquest. Originally, the castle was a Motte and Bailey type structure, quickly re-built of Caen stone and flint, as befitted an important fortification. Interestingly, the Saxons chose to guard the Arun gap from the opposite side of the river at Burpham, where fairly substantial earthworks indicate the remains of their fort.

When Roger de Montgomery's son Hugh died childless in 1094, the Castle passed to his troublesome brother, Robert de Belesme. He then had to forfeit the estate, for treason against Henry I and for a short period it

*Barbican, Arundel Castle*

remained in the hands of the Crown. By the 12th century, the Castle together with Earldom had been granted to the d'Albini family and was subsequently held by the Fitzalans. In 1556, Mary Fitzalan married Thomas Howard, fourth Duke of Norfolk, whose line still holds Arundel today.

The Castle has had three memorable sieges: the first, in 1102 when it was surrendered to Henry I: the second, in 1139 when it was besieged by Stephen: and the third, when it came under attack from the Parliamentary troops during the Civil War of 1643, when much of it was laid to ruins; the walls above the arch in the Barbican still bear the marks of the cannons. The Victorian Gothic reconstruction began some two hundred years later.

Arundel Castle together with the Fitzalan Chapel is open to visitors from the beginning of April until the end of October, Sundays to Fridays inclusive and there is an admission charge. This historic setting also provides a superb venue for a number of events throughout the year, including the Arundel Festival.

*The Keep, Arundel Castle*

# BOXGROVE PRIORY (6)

The village of Boxgrove lies between the A27 and the A285, about three and a half miles east of Chichester. The Priory is one of the most interesting ecclesiastical buildings in Sussex, yet it appears to be delightfully hidden down a narrow lane, off the main street in Boxgrove. It's somewhat of a surprise to round the corner and behold such an outstanding example of Norman architecture, tranquil and mellowed by the sunset.

Attached to the Abbey of Lessay in Normandy, the Benedictine Boxgrove Priory was founded by Robert de la Haye in the early part of the 12th century. It was enlarged several times over the years although it was served by only a few monks. After the dissolution of the monasteries in 1536, when Henry VIII quarrelled with the Pope, much of it fell into disrepair. The old Nave was demolished because the monks' church then became the Parish church. Prior to this, as was common with a Benedictine practise, the secular and clerical were separated.

The priory church, dedicated to St. Mary and St. Blaise, has been beautifully restored and the magnificent interior shows Norman to Early English features. There is a particularly splendid vaulted ceiling, intricately painted with leaves, flowers and berries, as well as many noteworthy monuments including an elaborate casket-shaped Chantry Chapel, the memorial to the 9th Lord de la Warr. Immediately behind the church are the ruins of the monastic quarters. From the site of the old Cloisters one passes the Chapter House; the monks' dormitory used to be above. Beyond are the substantial ruins of an entirely separate building, thought to be the Guest House or Prior's lodgings. Boxgrove Priory is open throughout the year and there is no admission to pay.

*The Guesthouse Ruins, Boxgrove Priory*

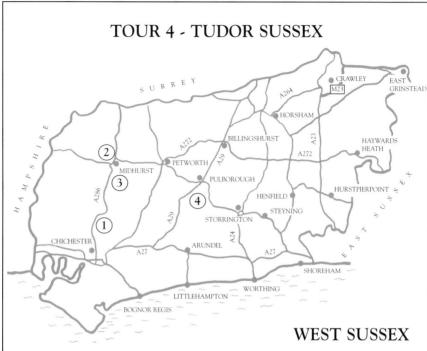

# TOUR 4 - TUDOR SUSSEX

SURREY

CRAWLEY
M23

EAST GRINSTEAD

HORSHAM

HAMPSHIRE

A272

BILLINGSHURST

A264

A23

HAYWARDS HEATH

②

MIDHURST

A286

③

PETWORTH

A29

PULBOROUGH

A272

HURSTPIERPOINT

④

HENFIELD

STEYNING

EAST SUSSEX

CHICHESTER

A29

STORRINGTON

①

ARUNDEL

A24

A27

A27

SHOREHAM

WORTHING

LITTLEHAMPTON

BOGNOR REGIS

## WEST SUSSEX

1. Weald and Downland Open Air Museum, Singleton
2. Midhurst

3. Cowdray Ruins, Midhurst
4. Parham House, Pulborough

*Weald and Downland Open Air Museum, Singleton*

22

# TOUR 4 - TUDOR SUSSEX

*The Tudor era reflects the years from 1485 until 1603. During that time, England witnessed five sovereigns; they were respectively: Henry VII from 1485: Henry VIII from 1509: Edward VI from 1547: Mary I from 1553 and finally, Elizabeth I from 1558. So much has been written about the Tudors, particularly the turbulent history of Henry VIII and then subsequently his youngest daughter, the wily Elizabeth who, when she eventually became Queen, ruled with equanimity.*

*During the latter Middle Ages the country generally prospered. Sussex saw a greatly increased demand in two areas of industry, iron working and shipbuilding, the Wealden forests being a source of material for both of these trades. There was an upsurge in building too, especially as the method of construction had undergone a revolutionary change. From a humble barn to an opulent manor, the framework was now made of massive timber beams with an in fill of bricks or wattle and daub. Naturally, the wood came from the rapidly decreasing Wealden forests. Another striking development was that of 'jettying' one floor over another. It offered a tremendous advantage in towns where space was valuable and it also gave added protection from the weather to the streets below. The attractively styled 'Wealden Hall House' became common to Sussex; here the main central hall was open to the roof and the jettied look often encircling the entire building. Today, although a number of Hall Houses have been beautifully preserved, others remain undiscovered because they're hopelessly altered and hidden behind younger facades.*

*The Tudor Tour gives an insight into our medieval architecture and the associated lifestyle. Start by visiting the fascinating Weald and Downland Open Air Museum at Singleton. Then spend a couple of hours at the ancient town of Midhurst and see if you can spot those Tudor gems. After a leisurely lunch, perhaps at the 16th century Spread Eagle Hotel, walk across the meadows to explore the ruins of the Tudor Cowdray House. Finally, if there's still an hour or two left of the day, why not drive to see the handsome Elizabethan Manor, Parham House, east of Pulborough.*

## WEALD & DOWNLAND OPEN AIR MUSEUM, SINGLETON (1)

Fifty acres of superb countryside provides the setting for a rich heritage of ancient buildings, saved from demolition in the Weald and Downland region. Founded in 1967 and opened to the public in 1971, the main object of this museum is to preserve those irreplaceable examples of architecture dating from medieval times through until the nineteenth century. With skilled handling, these buildings are dismantled and transported from their original sites and re-erected at Singleton, where they present the development of traditional construction throughout the centuries. The properties on view vary enormously: there's a medieval farmstead complete with a furnished farmhouse; a Victorian school: a granary: a working water mill and an aisled barn: a jettied 16th century market hall and timber framed shops, are all part of the town, which is still being formed.

The Weald and Downland Museum displays more than forty historic buildings which all contain their related information; special events take place throughout the season and visitors can watch some of the long established crafts being practised. Also within the grounds is a rustic little cafe serving rather yummy home-made fare. The attraction is open throughout the year, but from November until the end of February it's weekends and Wednesdays only. There is a fairly hefty admission charge but it's certainly very good value. Singleton is on the A286 about five miles north of Chichester.

## MIDHURST (2)

Positioned by the river in the exceptionally beautiful Rother Valley, Midhurst is undoubtedly one of the most picturesque towns in West Sussex. Yet, at first glance, it could almost be a victim of its own historic charm, for a surfeit of traffic frequently congests the wide High Street. With this in mind, its therefore preferable to head for the main Car Park on the northern side of the town, which is also handy for the Tourist Information Centre. Just a stone's throw from here the narrow medieval streets, with intimate little shops, have names such as Knockhundred Row, Duck Lane, Sheep lane and Wool Lane, all indicative of a bygone industry.

The history of this market town really begins in the 12th century when the Norman lord, Savaric Fitzcane built his castle on St. Ann's Hill, situated behind the church. A working community quickly sprang up around this fortified manor, the dwellings and market place being clustered at the foot of the hill. Over the centuries Midhurst changed and expanded and slowly, the evidence of our Norman ancestors disappeared; only the well preserved but scant remains of the castle still rest on the simple tree covered mound. Today, Midhurst provides us with later examples of 'living history'. The clutch of timbered 16th and 17th century buildings, constructed when it was a centre for weaving, mingle with some fine examples of Georgian architecture. A few, such as the Angel Hotel, had the Georgian style face-lift of adding a false and fashionable frontage. Two separate properties have been combined to make up the famous Spread Eagle Hotel; one part is 18th century, the other 17th century, with a beamed and jettied exterior; nearby is the Tudor Market Hall and the former Town Hall on whose northern side are the old Lock-up and Town Stocks. The Grammar School, founded in 1672 by Gilbert Hannan a local coverlet maker, can boast amongst its 'old boys', the writer H.G. Wells, the politician Richard Cobden and the geologist Charles Lyell.

Last, but not least (and by no means all) there's the Library on the corner of Knockhundred Row and Church Street. Once four cottages, the medieval interior of the beams, purlins and rafters are entirely open to view and, as it's a public building, a discreet glance inside should not go amiss.

## COWDRAY RUINS, MIDHURST (3)

From the entrance of the Car Park in Midhurst, a causeway leads across the water meadows to the River Rother and the impressive Cowdray ruins. At a distance the burnt-out shell looks eerily complete and it's only on closer examination that one realizes that the interior is open to the sky. This epitome of Tudor architecture, started at the beginning of the sixteenth century, took more than sixty years to complete under three different lords only to be gutted by fire in 1793.

*Cowdray ruins, Midhurst*

The building of Cowdray, the name being a derivation of 'la Coudraye', meaning a hazel copse, was begun by Sir David Owen. When he died in 1535, the great works continued under the Earl of Southampton, who had purchased Cowdray in 1529. On his death the estate passed to his half brother, Sir Anthony Browne, a great favourite of Henry VIII. Sir Anthony had been substantially rewarded by the King after the dissolution of the monasteries by being given Battle Abbey. At that point, a monk who had been evicted from the Abbey, placed a so-called curse on the Browne family, intimating they would perish by 'fire and water'. In 1793 his legendary curse came true when the eighth Viscount Montagne, descendant of Sir Anthony, drowned whilst trying to shoot the falls on the Rhine. He never knew that his beloved Cowdray had caught fire one week earlier and had become a pile of smouldering rubble with most of its contents destroyed.

The battlemented Cowdray ruins (sometimes called a castle), are open from April until the end of September, Friday to Tuesday inclusive and there is a small admission fee.

## PARHAM HOUSE, NEAR PULBOROUGH (4)

Set in park land facing a downland panorama, Parham is a classical Elizabethan house built in 1577 and having expansive gables, tall chimneys, mullioned windows and interior panelling. In 1540 Henry VIII granted the Manor of Parham to Robert Palmer, Mercer of London, whose two year old grandson laid the foundation stone of the present Parham House in 1577. The mother of this little boy happened to be a god-daughter of Queen Elizabeth I, who dined at Parham in 1593 on her way to Cowdray. Her Coat of Arms hangs in the Great Hall which has barely changed since she visited.

Over the years the house and gardens have been beautifully restored to reflect their 16th century grandeur and charm. The impressive rooms, which include the 160 foot Long Gallery, are filled with a unique collection of paintings, tapestries and furniture. Parham is situated on the A283 between Pulborough and Storrington and is open to the public on Wednesdays, Thursdays and Sundays, from April until the end of October. There is an entrance charge.

*Parham House*

# TOUR 5 - AN INDUSTRIAL ERA

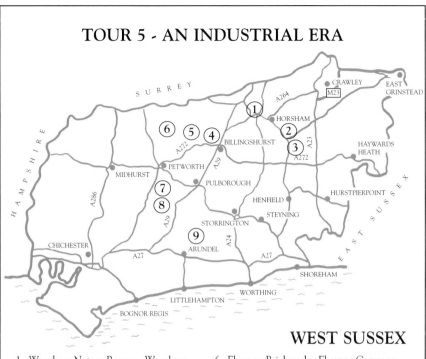

## WEST SUSSEX

1. Warnham Nature Reserve, Warnham
2. Hammer Ponds, Bucks Head
3. Leonardslee Gardens, Horsham
4. Wisborough Green
5. Kirdford
6. Ebernoe Brickworks, Ebernoe Common
7. Coultershaw Beam Pump
8. Burton Mill Ponds, nr Petworth
9. Amberley Chalk Pits Museum, Amberley

*The Village Sign, Kirdford*

# TOUR 5 - AN INDUSTRIAL ERA

*Tour the old industrial sites in the upper regions of West Sussex and see the dramatic change that has been wrought on the barren wilderness of the 16th century, when the great forests were literally swallowed up to feed the fires of the iron furnaces and, latterly, glass furnaces too. Watch the wildlife that inhabits the lakes and ponds, artificially created nearly five hundred years ago, to provide water power to drive the bellows and hammers needed for iron smelting. Visit the brick kilns that functioned for two hundred years and are now derelict and hidden amongst the trees of a nature reserve.*

*Iron has been worked in Sussex since Roman times: the method changed little over the years. Around 1500, a more effective operation was introduced from Europe, which coincided with an increased demand for iron. The instant profits that could be made beckoned the landowners and Iron Masters and little thought was given to the landscape. Streams were dammed to make hammer ponds. Huge stone lined furnaces were built. Shacks were erected and trees were felled at such an alarming rate, it caused national concern. A busy furnace could burn about 5000 tons of wood a year. The 16th century also saw an explosion in the glass industry. Several furnaces were established north of Petworth by the Huguenot glassworkers from France. They too, needed fuel for their furnaces. For fifty years or more, competition was keen between the two industries for the available wood. Iron won eventually: for in 1615 an Act was passed prohibiting the felling of trees for glass making.*

*Less than a hundred years later, coal was discovered in the Midlands. It was a great deal cheaper to burn than wood, so fortunately for the Sussex countryside the iron foundries gradually moved to the north where the coal was mined.*

## WARNHAM NATURE RESERVE, HORSHAM (1)

Indicated from the A24 on the northern perimeter of Horsham, Warnham Nature Reserve now surrounds Warnham Mill Pond. Originally a 'hammer pond', the 15 acre lake was created for the iron industry of the 16th century. The ironworks were later destroyed during the Civil War of 1644. At the end of the 17th century a flour mill was built on the site, which remained operational until the 1930's.

Before heading off along one of the footpaths to explore the Reserve, why not pop into the Visitor Centre first; it contains detailed information on the area and all its associated wildlife.

## HAMMER PONDS, BUCKS HEAD (2)

Hawkins Pond and Hammer Pond; two great lakes created to fulfil the insatiable demands for more and more iron. Situated in what was once the densely wooded St. Leonards Forest, these silent but beautiful reminders of the past, have a low hill dividing them. The lakes are placed by the minor road to Bucks Head. This is south east of Horsham off the A281.

## LEONARDSLEE GARDENS, HORSHAM (3)

Tall Pines, Maples and the vivid hues of Azaleas and Rhododendrons are just some of nature's wonders that surround the lakes and waterfalls of Leonardslee Gardens.

Landscaped by Sir Edmund Loder in 1889, the 240 acres have been improved over the years and is now established as one of the finest gardens in the world.

Pause for a minute or two as you look at this delightful scenery and let your imagination travel back for four hundred years. Not a spot of colour would have nudged the lakes then: nor would a tree have pierced the skyline. Instead, the murky water would have been surrounded by the sheds, forges and machinery, necessary for iron smelting. The soil would have been bare and rutted from overuse and all the while, the acrid smell of the fires, devouring every tree, would have hung in the air.

Leonardslee is situated about five miles south-east of Horsham on the A281. It's open from the beginning of April until the end of October and there is an entrance charge.

## WISBOROUGH GREEN (4)

Even the over subscribed A272 to Petworth, which passes the perimeter of Wisborough Green, doesn't really spoil this beautiful village. Set in rolling countryside the cottages, steeped in history, are immaculately kept and encircle the

*Church of St Peter's, Wisborough Green*

tree-lined village green. The hanging baskets are filled to perfection; there is a fine church of Norman origin; a pretty pond, good pubs and throughout the summer those, oh so English, cricket matches take place on the green. Yet the chocolate box prettiness belies the past years of Wisborough Green; for this area was the industrial heart of glassworking until the 17th century and those desirable cottages were tumbledown dwellings belonging to the glassworkers and their families.

Do ensure a visit to the Church of St. Peter's Ad Vincula. Here the tiny window at the end of the south wall is composed of 16th century glass, made by the local Huguenot glass makers, refugees of the Wars of Religion in France. The wording at the base of the glass reads:-

"This glass made locally - circa 1600, commemorates the principal Glassworkers in this parish: the Bongars and Caquerays from Normandy and the Hennezils and Thietrys from Lorraine. Dedicated 1968."

## KIRDFORD (5)

Every wall in Kirdford appears to be clad in the most wonderful climbing roses and almost every available field is transformed into an orchard; for Kirdford's industry today is apple growing. Not a trace of those 16th century glassworks remains and supposedly, there were eight within this parish alone

Yet stop and have a close look at the village sign, erected in 1937 to commemorate the Coronation of George VI and Queen Elizabeth. The diamond panes of glass at the top, are indicative of the local glass industry and the sign on the plinth below gives a potted history of Kirdford from the Bronze Age through to modern times.

One interesting glass furnace was discovered at the nearby Slifehurst Farm during the 1930's. It was exposed when a field drain was being cut and revealed lumps of glass and a sixteen foot long sandstone floor, covered with a layer of charcoal. The church with its solid 15th century tower contains a lancet window, glazed in 1933 with richly coloured fragments of local glass. Kirdford lies about two miles north-west of Wisborough Green.

## EBERNOE BRICKWORKS, EBERNOE COMMON (6)

Ebernoe Common, a large area of woodland used for many hundreds of years by villagers for grazing livestock, is now a reserve owned by The Sussex Trust for Nature Conservation. Twice it has been a fairly major industrial site. Initially this was in the 16th century, when it was used for iron working. Now the old hammer pond of yesteryear lies serenely in a hollow covered with water lilies and screened by oaks and beeches.

Ebernoe brickworks were established at the beginning of the 18th century, long after the production of iron had ceased here, although there is some evidence of bricks being supplied to Petworth from this site even earlier. The layout of the brickworks is indicated on a map of 1829 and they remained unaltered until their closure in the 1930's.

*Ebernoe Brickworks*

Ebernoe proved to be an ideal site for brick working as clay was plentiful and easily dug from the surrounding area. After digging, the clay was conveyed to the pug mill where, mixed with water from the pond, it became malleable. Afterwards, the substance was taken to the moulding shed to be fashioned by hand into tiles or bricks: these were then dried and fired in the kilns.

Today, the substantial remains of the kiln and the moulding shed peer facelessly through the woodland, offering an interesting insight into an industry that is now mechanized. There is an excellent information board on the moulding shed wall. Ebernoe is not that easy to find. It lies on a minor road, just east of the A283, between Petworth and Northchapel. Follow the signs to the church, where there is adequate car parking. The entrance to Ebernoe Common is situated between the church and the Old School House.

## COULTERSHAW BEAM PUMP (7)

The Coultershaw Beam Pump lies a couple of miles south of Petworth, close to Coultershaw Bridge. This scheduled ancient monument was first installed in the 18th century by the Earl of Egremont to pump water from the River Rother to Petworth. Now fully restored by The Sussex Archeological Society, this particular beam pump was cast in the mid 19th century and worked until 1960. The building also houses other beam pumps, a history of pumping and the Rother navigation plus information on the Coultershaw locality. Coultershaw Beam Pump is open on the 1st and 3rd Sunday of each month from April until September.

## BURTON MILL PONDS, NEAR PETWORTH (8)

Discover the lovely, yet secretive tract of water, Burton Mill Pond. It was originally a huge hammer pond for the most southerly iron works in West Sussex. The restored Mill House, built about 1780, is not open to the public, but there are some very pretty footpaths that meander along the western edge of the mill pond. They are all signed and there's plenty of parking by the Mill House. Burton Mill is indicated from the A285 about two and a half miles south of Petworth.

## AMBERLEY CHALK PITS MUSEUM, AMBERLEY (9)

The Industrial Tour wouldn't be complete without visiting the industrial museum of the south, Amberley Chalk Pits. Here the past (and some present) industries of Sussex are reconstructed on a thirty-six acre site, positioned amongst the workings of an old chalk pit, last used in 1960. You can see the craftsmen at work; the blacksmith in his forge; the potter at his wheel and the wood turner's workshop. There are exhibitions on the Wealden ironworking and brickmaking. Browse amongst a tools and trades history display or ride on the narrow gauge railway. These are just a few of the things to do and see at Amberley Museum, which is open from mid March until the beginning of November, Wednesday to Sunday. There is an admission charge and it's situated on the B2139 next to Amberley railway station.

# TOUR 6 - BRIDGE HOPPING DOWN THE ARUN

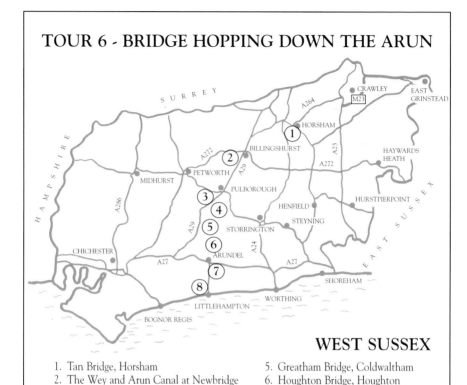

## WEST SUSSEX

1. Tan Bridge, Horsham
2. The Wey and Arun Canal at Newbridge
3. Stopham Bridge, Stopham
4. The Old Bridge, Pulborough

5. Greatham Bridge, Coldwaltham
6. Houghton Bridge, Houghton
7. Arundel Bridge, Arundel
8. The Bridges at Littlehampton

*Stopham Bridge*

# TOUR 6 - BRIDGE HOPPING DOWN THE ARUN

*The Arun is one of the longest Sussex rivers and its humble beginnings are situated in the beautiful surroundings of St. Leonard's Forest, east of Horsham. Three tributaries, including the Rother (see Tour 7), plus a multitude of subsidiary brooks combine to form the Arun, whose meandering course finally reaches the sea at Littlehampton. From the forest source, the river flows southwards around Horsham and then perambulates through rolling countryside, passing Billingshurst, Pulborough and Arundel on the way.*

*To cover as much of the Arun as possible, the tour 'bridge hops' and visits several of the old stone bridges that cross the course of this ancient waterway. From each of these points you can discover the surrounding history, wildlife and walks. Some of the bridges have pubs within the immediate vicinity, but I think it's rather pleasant to take a picnic, find a quiet spot and enjoy the unspoilt riverside locality.*

## TAN BRIDGE, HORSHAM (1)

Tan Bridge crosses the Arun not far south of Carfax, Horsham's busy town centre and the Causeway, a tree-lined district with ancient buildings, Horsham Museum and the Town Hall. Close by is the delightful 13th century church of St. Mary, whose Gardens of Remembrance dally with the nearby meadowland. Tan Bridge acquired its name from the tanning industry that prospered hereabouts during the 13th and 14th centuries. Apparently the tanning of leather, which needed a lot of water, also created foul smells and it was considered necessary to site the industry outside the borough, on the far side of the river.

The Horsham Society in conjunction with Horsham District Council produce an excellent leaflet entitled 'Horsham Riverside Walk'. This is an interesting nine mile route encircling Horsham and for the majority of the way following the River Arun, the Red River or various brooks. The leaflet, which can be obtained from the Tourist Information Centre, indicates the entire walk plus the wheelchair friendly sections, the parking spots and the points of interest.

## THE WEY AND ARUN CANAL AT NEWBRIDGE (2)

The Wey and Arun Canal was constructed to link the rivers of the same names to form an inland waterway. The concept of the canal link was to provide cheap and easy access for the delivery of coal, chalk, agricultural produce and other goods to parts of Sussex, Surrey and London. The river up to Arundel was navigable by ships as early as the 1550's; small vessels were able to get to Houghton Bridge beyond. By 1787, further work had improved the stretch up to Pallingham Quay and then subsequently to Newbridge. The final link was completed in 1816. The building of the railways during the 19th century, led to a gradual abandonment of the canals as the transportation of freight became even easier by train. By 1871 the Wey and Arun Canal had been formally closed.

Since 1970, the Wey and Arun Canal Trust has been actively restoring 'London's lost route to the sea' for recreational purposes. The Trust offers public cruises at weekends during the season on a 50 ft narrow boat along certain stretches

*Newbridge*

of the canal. For details and information, phone (01403) 752403.

The name 'Newbridge' probably arises from a 'New Bridge' being built to cross the Arun. The present bridge is supposed to encapsulate an older one within and the pleasant pastoral towpath either side, enables one to see the structure in its entirety. There's no doubt in my mind that the footpath leading to the south and eventually to Stopham Bridge, covers one of the loveliest and wildest areas of the Arun. It's a seven mile stretch and if you're thinking of walking it, do note that it's essential to consult the Ordnance Survey Pathfinder maps 1267 and 1287 before setting out. The track zigzags in a complicated fashion, sometimes following the river, sometimes the canal and sometimes passing through woods and fields. Newbridge is located between Billingshurst and Wisborough Green on the A272.

## STOPHAM BRIDGE, STOPHAM (3)

A magnificent medieval bridge positioned just above the meeting place of the Rother and Arun rivers. Built of stone, the bridge has seven semicircular arches, with the central one being raised to allow masted vessels access. A series of pedestrian passing places (two persons at a squash), are on either side. It must have been the bain of every motorist's life to cross Stopham Bridge; it was, after all, meant for horses and therefore could only manage one-way traffic. Fortunately (for the bridge in particular), by 1986 a modern version had been erected just to the north, leaving the old one preserved and deservedly a Scheduled Ancient Monument.

With Stopham Bridge now bypassed, the old road is only open for access to view the series of medieval arches that span the Arun and, wait for it ....... to reach The White Hart, a picturesque pub which, in the summer, uses the former highway for extra tables. Stopham is located by the A283 about one mile west of Pulborough.

## THE OLD BRIDGE, PULBOROUGH (4)

A scattered town whose historical heyday was during the Roman occupation (see Roman Sussex). However, here and there are pockets of a more recent past with buildings dating from Tudor times onwards. The Arun flows immediately to the south of the town and although the modern bridge that crosses it is not displeasing, it's situated far too close to the 18th century companion, which looks remarkably like a pared down version of Stopham Bridge.

From here, look south eastwards across to Pulborough Brooks Nature Reserve at Wiggenholt. The reserve which roughly covers four hundred acres, mostly in the Arun Valley, is being re-established by the Royal Society for The Protection of Birds as an area of national importance for birds and other wildlife. The Upperton Barn Visitor Centre at Wiggenholt contains a wealth of ornithology related information as well as a powerful telescope, positioned against picture windows, for visitors to scan the marshy terrain in detail.

There are a number of wildlife walks around the Reserve and some of these can be negotiated by a wheelchair. Pulborough Brooks is open daily throughout the year and is indicated from the A283, south of Pulborough. (01798) 875851.

## GREATHAM BRIDGE, NEAR COLDWALTHAM (5)

Greatham Bridge is situated in lonely marshland on a minor road, linking the A29 at Coldwaltham to the A283 beyond the hamlet of Greatham. In early times, when the Arun was broader, this particular stretch could only be negotiated by ferry. Eventually a lengthy bridge was built to ford the river, but in later years this has obviously had problems, because a rather ugly steel section has been incorporated with the old stonework. The footpath on the far side of the river travels directly southwards across Amberley Wild Brooks, a nature reserve managed by The Sussex Trust for Nature Conservation. The walk across the brooks, which are frequently flooded in winter, is about two miles and leads to the enchanting village of Amberley.

*Greatham Bridge*

## HOUGHTON BRIDGE, HOUGHTON (6)

Interestingly sited on a bend in the river below steep downland, the weathered stonework of Houghton Bridge appears to be of medieval origin; in fact it replaced the older version in 1875. This pretty little section of the Arun is one of contrasts and has attracted the visitor for a number of years. On one side of the river the Downs nudge the meanders and a worked out quarry provides a site for Amberley Chalk Pits Museum (see Industrial Sussex). On the other side are broad pastures with riverside walks and a few pleasure craft, sometimes vying for a mooring with the swans. Adjacent to the bridge is an inn, a tea rooms and a tiny Toll House.

*Houghton Bridge, Houghton*

Houghton itself is one long street (the B2139), with a 13th century church, simple but attractive cottages and The George and Dragon Inn. Supposedly, Charles II stopped here for a pint when he was on his way to Brighton to board a boat for France.

## ARUNDEL BRIDGE, ARUNDEL (7)

How many thousands of years did it take the Arun to carve its way through the downland to Arundel? Or was it, as the experts often suggest, simply an enormous estuary stretching inland to Pulborough that narrowed to a river with evolution. We can only look .... and imagine.

From Houghton Bridge the river goes on to form a loop round North Stoke, pass its counterpart South Stoke on the opposite side and with another loop, touch the village of Burpham before doubling back on itself to reach Arundel and Arundel Castle (see Norman Sussex). The date of Arundel's first bridge is uncertain. Presumably a wooden structure, it could have been during Roman times when all roads leading to Chichester were of great importance; or Saxon times when a substantial Saxon fort lay upstream at Burpham; or it could have been after the Norman Conquest, coinciding with the building of the Castle. Records suggest that by the 18th century Arundel had at last become the proud owner of an impressive stone bridge. This was replaced after two hundred years to cope with the ever increasing traffic.

## THE BRIDGES AT LITTLEHAMPTON (8)

Having negotiated the flat coastal plain from Arundel, the river enters the sea at Littlehampton. The road bridge is on the western outskirts, but the modern footbridge is much closer to the mouth. This was built on the site of the former chain ferry (1825) and swing bridge (1908) and links the old town to the sandy dunes of the West Beach, a haven for wildlife and seashore plants.

At the beginning of the 19th century, Littlehampton was a fishing village and small port that grew into a popular seaside resort during the Victorian and Edwardian eras. Although it has continued to mushroom, the town appears to have been left behind compared to its neighbour, Worthing; yet this has somehow given it an indefinable charm, which makes it an ideal place for those traditional family holidays. Sited by the promenade, there's the joyous attraction (for the kids anyway) of an amusement park. There's the Old Town to explore, where the irregular streets hold a mixture of Sussex flint and pebble cottages and 18th/19th/20th century buildings. Positioned along the river are the former wharves, warehouses and shipyards, now used for boat building, as well as a very busy marina. In Church Street, Littlehampton Museum contains informative displays on the history of the town and the surrounding area. It's open throughout the year from Tuesday to Saturday and the admission is free.

# TOUR 7 - THE VILLAGES OF THE ROTHER

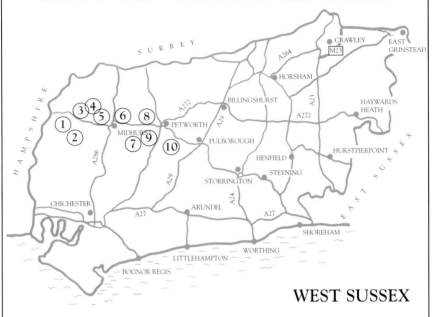

## WEST SUSSEX

1. Rogate
2. Trotton
3. Chithurst
4. Iping
5. Stedham
6. Easebourne
7. Selham
8. Lodsworth
9. Tillington
10. Fittleworth

*Crossing the Rother at Fittleworth*

# TOUR 7 - THE VILLAGES OF THE ROTHER

*Confusingly there are two River Rothers, one in East Sussex and this one in West Sussex, known as the 'little' or 'western' Rother. In reality, the Little Rother is more of a major tributary, for it flows into the River Arun just east of Fittleworth, near Pulborough; its meandering journey through the County covering somewhere in the region of twenty-five miles.*

*When this tour joins the river at Rogate, close to the Hampshire border, the Rother has already started to travel eastwards through an expansive valley with downland to the south and the wooded slopes of the Weald to the north. It flows around the busy market town of Midhurst and manages to by-pass Petworth; otherwise the watery passage is beautifully rural and unhurried, the only interruptions being weirs and medieval bridges, a few picturesque villages, a few historic churches and a few good pubs.*

## ROGATE (1)

A pleasant sandstone village by the A272 in the extreme west of the County. The Church of St. Bartholomew has been fairly heavily restored, but the interior retains some 13th century features and an unusual shingled bell tower. About a mile and a half to the west, yet again, are the scanty remains of Durford Abbey, a house of Premonstratensian Canons founded in the 12th century by Henry de Hoese. The canons were responsible for the building and the maintenance of three bridges across the Rother, including Durford Bridge just east of the Abbey.

## TROTTON (2)

Trotton claims one of the loveliest medieval bridges in Sussex, yet all the unsuitable A272 traffic races across the antiquated structure, making it difficult to appreciate, never mind getting a decent photograph. Built of stone by Lord Camoys in the early

*The Church of St George, Trotton*   *Wall Paintings, St George's Church, Trotton*

15th century, it has five arches with cutwaters on either side. Lord Camoys (a hero of Agincourt) and his family, once Lords of the Manor, have two commemorative brasses in the Parish Church of St. George adjacent to the bridge. Internally, the church features a number of notable red ochre wall paintings dating from the 14th century; these include the Seven Acts of Mercy, the Seven Deadly Sins and the Last Judgement. There is some parking opposite the church and from here a bridlepath leads through meadowland finishing at the mill and weir at Dumpford. It's about 1/2 mile and makes a pleasant little stroll. The Keepers Arms, tucked on high ground by the main road is well recommended and do take a look at the Dried Flower Barn on the other side of the lane.

## CHITHURST (3)

Until Midhurst, the Rother perambulates for a while to the north of the A272. It appears that almost every Rother village is blessed with a picture postcard bridge and Chithurst is no exception. Here the twin arches are fringed with willows, lush gardens and a steep hillock surmounted by a simple 11th century church. Note Chithurst Abbey to the west of the church.

On leaving Chithurst continue northwards by way of a narrow lane which takes a sharp right turn. This is Hammer Lane and after about half a mile stop for a short but historical walk in Hammer Woods. The stream to the right is Hammer Stream and if you follow the bridlepath on the left, it will take you past Hammer Pond: all left over relics of the 16th century iron industry that once flourished hereabouts. Oh and by the way, north of Hammer Pond are the remains of an Iron Age fort.

## IPING (4)

Yet another five arched stone bridge spans the Rother at Iping, very close to the old water mill. Immediately to the south of this is a bridlepath on the left which offers an attractive riverside walk of 3/4 mile through to Stedham. Crossing the river about 1/4 mile to the west of Iping and continuing towards Iping Common, is the route of the old Roman road leading from Chichester to Silchester, in Hampshire.

## STEDHAM (5)

Having returned to the A272, a sign appears almost instantaneously indicating Stedham one of the larger Rother villages. A good old British pub is the first thing that meets the eye; yet this is no ordinary pub, for the cuisine is Thai and whilst beer, sausage and chips are still served alongside, Thai food makes up the greater part of the menu. The place was packed, so I think that possibly speaks for itself. Stedham's 17th century bridge lies on the northern perimeter and is reached by a long street of mellow brick cottages. Beyond the substantial village green are the Victorian church and Stedham Hall whose handsome Tudor style facade is mostly 20th century.

## EASEBOURNE (6)

More of a hamlet than a village, Woolbeding is passed on the way to Easebourne. There is simply a church, the 18th century Woolbeding Hall and a medieval bridge, about half a mile to the south.

The remains of Easebourne's 13th century Priory are now incorporated with St Mary's Church and other buildings. The nuns obviously had quite reputation, for in the 15th century the Prioress was found guilty of extravagance and 'not so saintly' living; she was duly suspended. The bright yellow paintwork on the properties in this area, indicate ownership by the 17,000 acre Cowdray Estate, one of the largest in Sussex. The ruins of Cowdray Castle are situated south of Easebourne in Cowdray Park and the history is covered in 'Tudor Sussex'.

## SELHAM (7)

Follow the A286 road through Midhurst then take the road to the east that runs past the hamlet of West Lavington. This is an extremely pretty route with glorious views across the river and Cowdray Park to Cowdray House. In spite of Selham being scattered with no apparent centre, it has a pub with the curious name of The Three Moles and an interesting church. This ecclesiastical building poses a bit of a puzzler for the experts, who seem uncertain if its beginnings are Saxon or Norman; yet the weird carvings of snakes and monsters are of Viking manner! South of Selham is the dismantled Midhurst to Pulborough railway line closed, like others, with the axe wielded during the 1960's.

## LODSWORTH (8)

On sloping ground the well laid out village of Lodsworth has an impressive prospect across the Rother Valley. The old cottages are well restored with enviably flourishing gardens; presumably the soil is right for growing anything and everything. Look for the 18th century Dower House, a handsome three storeyed structure and its younger neighbour, The Great House.

## TILLINGTON (9)

Set back from the A272 and before reaching Tillington is The Manor of Dean. This delightful 17th century building whose landscaped gardens, containing a variety of flowers, shrubs and specimen trees, are open to visitors on a number of occasions throughout the year in aid of the National Gardens Scheme. For the appropriate details or booklet on the opening times contact any Tourist Information Centre. The immaculate village of Tillington sits on a high ridge west of Petworth, much of it belonging to the Petworth estate. The church boasts a peculiarly graceful Scots Crown tower, which was included in Turner's landscape paintings of the area.

## FITTLEWORTH (10)

The last (or the first) and I think my favourite village in this tour of the Rother. Fittleworth has long been the haunt of artists and writers and 'tis said, Edward Elgar spent a summer here composing great musical works. Medieval timber framed cottages are tucked against the rocky outcrop of sandstone, beech and oak trees. The 14th century tile hung Swan Inn is warm and inviting, beckoning the anglers who fish by the Tudor bridge a few yards away. For those who want an end of day amble along the river bank, then Fittleworth is the place to be.

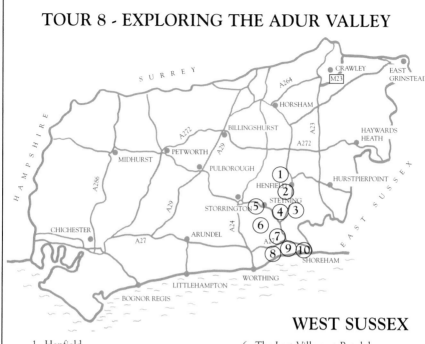

# TOUR 8 - EXPLORING THE ADUR VALLEY

## WEST SUSSEX

1. Henfield
2. The Downs Link
3. Woods Mill, Small Dole
4. Bramber
5. Steyning

6. The Lost Village at Botolphs
7. Lancing College Chapel, Lancing
8. Shoreham Airport
9. Old Shoreham
10. New Shoreham

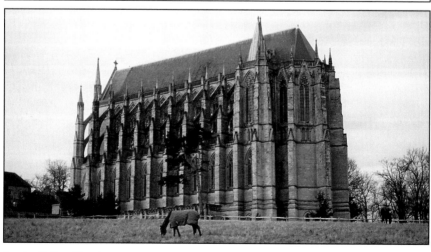

*Lancing College Chapel*

42

# TOUR 8 - EXPLORING THE ADUR VALLEY

*The River Adur has two sources, one is the western Adur which rises in the parish of Slinfold, the other is the eastern Adur, rising near Burgess Hill. The two meet in the marshy plains near Henfield and then take a common route, (about 8 miles as the crow flies) through the Adur valley entering the sea at Shoreham. Except for Shoreham, the Adur has no major towns on its course and passes very few villages. But the passage from Henfield levels through the gap in the chalk Downs is an interesting one.*

*So why not join me at Henfield to explore this river's past history and present attractions as it journeys unhurriedly towards the sea.*

## HENFIELD (1)

Henfield lies three miles west of the A23 and is located on the A281, once part of the old London - Brighton stage-coach route. In spite of its growth and a number of trendier shops, the village atmosphere has been successfully retained. The name is a play on a Saxon word meaning 'a settlement on open ground' and the artifacts discovered so far indicate both the Saxons, and previously the Romans, occupied this area. For an in-depth look at Henfield's history, pop into the museum housed in the Village Hall. It contains an extensive collection of local material, including paintings and old photographs; admission is free and it's open from 10.00 a.m. to 12 noon, Monday, Tuesday, Thursday and Saturday, then 2.30 p.m. to 4.30 p.m. on Wednesday.

The 13th century church is constructed on Saxon foundations and tucked away from the main street down a road that eventually culminates in several footpaths, all leading across the water meadows to the Adur. Don't miss seeing the 16th century Cat House whose exterior is decorated with cats. The legend suggests the one-time occupants were fed up with the vicar's carnivorous cat because he'd pinched their canary. Presumably, they hoped that by fixing feline replicas outside it would, if possible, scare him to death!

## THE DOWNS LINK (2)

Established in 1984, the Downs Link provides a continual network of footpaths and bridleways linking the North Downs Way in Surrey with the South Downs Way in West Sussex. Having met the South Downs Way near Steyning, it then becomes the Coastal Link and continues by the River Adur to Shoreham. Wherever possible the Downs Link follows disused railway tracks and its entry into Henfield is via the old Horsham to Shoreham railway opened in 1861 and closed in the mid 1960's. The path can be joined in Henfield by the old Station Hotel (now The Cat and The Canary); it then goes on to zig-zag through the Adur Valley. If you felt inclined, it would be perfectly feasible to do this tour on foot, on a bike or even on a horse, but it would take a little longer. For further information about the Downs Link telephone (01243) 777610.

## WOODS MILL, SMALL DOLE (3)

Two miles south of Henfield on the A2037, is a handsome 18th century water mill, which became the headquarters of the Sussex Wildlife Trust in 1966. The Trust, formed in 1961, is designed to acquire and manage land in Sussex as Nature Reserves for the benefit of both wildlife and people. Their fifteen acre Reserve that surrounds Woods Mill has some informative nature trails through woodland, meadow and marsh. Special events and guided walks are held throughout the season and the mill itself keeps an exhibition on the natural history of the area. For details on opening times telephone (01273) 492630.

## BRAMBER (4)

Pass through the gap in the Downs (carved by the river over thousands of years), cross the Adur and you're in Bramber. From here it's easy to see how the village formed around Bramber Castle (see Norman Sussex), whose remaining wall of the Keep still lords over the domain and looks more like a folly. Note the timber framed property on the left, just after crossing the bridge. This is St. Mary's c. 1470, originally built for the monks of Sele Priory at Beeding, as a guest house for pilgrims on their way to Chichester. The monks were also responsible for the upkeep of the former stone bridge that supposedly had a chapel in the centre. St. Mary's, which is still lived in, has a unique Elizabethan painted room and attractive gardens. It's open from Easter until the end of September, Sundays and Thursdays, p.m. only.

*St Mary's, Bramber*

The rest of Bramber's ancient High Street is well preserved and will delight the visitor, who might try and let his, or her, imagination stretch back to the 11th century. In those days the river was navigable for several miles upstream and Bramber, together with Steyning were busy ports and shipbuilding centres, positioned on a wide estuary. Disaster struck when due to silting up, the river could no longer accommodate large vessels. Bramber and Steyning saw their fortunes decline as a replacement port had to be built at Old Shoreham.

# STEYNING (5)

It's difficult to know whether to describe Steyning as a little town or a large village. However, there's no doubt it's medieval core has some of the finest examples of domestic architecture in West Sussex. First settled in by the Romans, Steyning then became a sizeable Saxon community with a port and a mint; examples of the coins minted can be found in Brighton Museum. After the sea receded its prosperity waned, until it became re-established as a thriving market town a couple of hundred years later.

At least an hour or two needs to be spent discovering Steyning's curving streets and medley of historic buildings. You'll find Tudor and Carolean styles happily rubbing noses with their Georgian or Victorian counterparts. Look for the old Grammar School in Church Street, established in 1614 and housed in a marvellous timber framed and jettied structure: the Prison House on the corner of the High Street is thought to cover the site of the Saxon Mint: Old Market House, once used by Quakers, is tile hung with a curious little clock turret: the 15th century Chequer Inn, a one time coaching hostelry, or the handsome 17th century Norfolk Arms make a notable setting for a lunch break. The rather grand church of St. Andrew, founded in the 8th century by St. Cuthman, was built by the monks of Fecamp in 1047 after it was given to them by Edward the Confessor. Finally, don't forget to visit Steyning Museum. It has a wealth of information about the town's eventful history and admission is free. It's open all the year from Tuesdays to Saturdays, 10.30 a.m. to 12.30 p.m. and 2.30 to 4.30 p.m.

## THE LOST VILLAGE AT BOTOLPHS (6)

Showing many Saxon features, the little church at Botolphs serves as a reminder that its former village, called Annington, was de-populated by the Black Death. At Domesday the community had over thirty smallholders and a number of villagers. The rustic church is well worth a visit and to reach Botolphs and subsequently Lancing Chapel, take the minor road from Steyning southwards towards the A27. This traverses the western side of the river.

## LANCING COLLEGE CHAPEL, LANCING (7)

It's the chapel, not the school, which is the dominating feature of the Adur landscape and whilst not pretty, it's certainly an impressive example of 19th century Gothic architecture. Don't be put off by the slightly forbidding facade. The interior is atmospheric simplicity, enhanced by beautiful stained glass and intricately worked tapestries.

Lancing College is an independent school founded by Nathaniel Woodard, Curate at Shoreham in 1848 and it was to be one of the first of several schools he established. The construction of the chapel began in 1868. It's built of Sussex sandstone and foundations of up to seventy feet deep ensure a firm hold on the chapel's hillside position. Maintenance and restoration are ongoing tasks. Lancing Chapel is open daily to visitors, but on Sundays it's 12 noon to 4 p.m. only.

## SHOREHAM AIRPORT (8)

Shoreham Airport lies on the southern side of the A27, more or less opposite Lancing College. Established in 1910, it has become the earliest surviving Civil

Airport in the world and today provides a major base for flying activities on the south coast. Being a public airport it's great fun to spend a little time here, watching the 'comings and goings' of air bound traffic from the viewing gallery. The original Art Deco terminal has a good bar and restaurant and the terminal shop offers a range of aviation based products for sale. Guided airport tours can also be organized and what's more .... the parking is free.

## OLD SHOREHAM (9)

What a delight Old Shoreham must have been and what a shame it's now encircled by suburbia. Nevertheless, if you leave your car by the church and take short walk you can still enjoy some of the past features.

For a spell Old Shoreham became the main village and port on the Adur, after the silting up of Bramber. According to the Domesday Book there were more than seventy people living in Old Shoreham and probably most worked at the port. By about 1100, due to the ongoing coastal erosion, the port had to be moved southwards once more, this time to New Shoreham at the mouth of the river. The charming church of St. Nicholas is basically Saxon and the squat tower that rises above the remaining fishermen's cottages, overlooks the river and the old timber toll bridge. This was built in 1781 to replace the ferry and was only closed to traffic in 1970. It has now become a footbridge giving access to riverside walks with some wonderful views up and down stream.

## NEW SHOREHAM (10)

The planning and building of New Shoreham began around 1100 AD. It was to be a sizeable Norman port with a town and a central church of cathedral like proportions. St. Mary de Haura, built between 1100 - 1130 AD, is today half its original length; 100 feet instead of 200 feet. At some point a part of the nave fell into a derelict state and by 1720 had simply been blocked up. The ruins are still visible in the churchyard.

There are some buildings of great antiquity in New Shoreham, but like Old Shoreham and for the same reason, the charm is rather dissipated; yet it still bears an exciting, if slightly faded aura of a seaside port. In the High Street the curiously chequer-worked Marlipins Museum has walls constructed of knapped flint and Caen stone. Thought to be the oldest secular building in this country, it was used as a Norman customs house for the de Broase family of Bramber. Today, the museum is owned by The Sussex Archeological Society who maintain some excellent exhibits on the general history of the area. It's open from May to September inclusive and there is a small entrance charge.

Opposite Marlipins the frontage of The Crown and Anchor sports a large overhanging figure of a roguish sailor. Nearby a footbridge crosses the harbour and links New Shoreham to the chalet type estate of Shoreham Beach on whose eastern end is Shoreham Fort, a part of England's defence system built in the 1850's. Finally if you look towards Brighton, you'll see the ongoing stretch of Shoreham's new harbour, now one of the main ports for the south coast.

*Marlipins Museum, New Shoreham*

# TOUR 9 - FLORA AND FAUNA

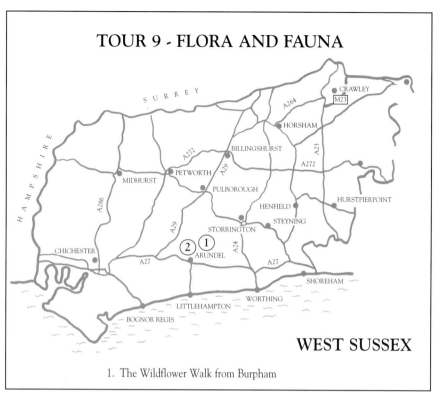

## WEST SUSSEX

1. The Wildflower Walk from Burpham

*View from Burpham to Arundel Castle*

# TOUR 9 - FLORA AND FAUNA

*There is only one way to appreciate the Flora and Fauna of any area and that's on foot; so when the barometer has crept up to 'Fine' and the TV weather man is all smiles, park the car in a suitable place (in this case the Car Park conveniently close to the 'George and Dragon' pub) and get walking.*

*This circular 3 1/4 mile route starts in the pretty little village of Burpham situated on the lower slopes of the Downs, above the Arun valley. The walk is unusual, for it covers three very different aspects of the West Sussex landscape and therefore, the related wildlife. Initially the path meanders by the peaceful River Arun, where the reeded banks provide a haven for water birds and the rich damp soil of the water-meadows produces a mass of flowers. Next, it wanders through woodland where the clumsy tracks of badgers weave beneath the delicate blooms of blackthorn and heedlessly through the bluebells. Finally, the trail perambulates across the chalk Downs and here the springy turf sprinkled with tiny flowers, together with broad views and the song of the lark, epitomizes Sussex.*

*....... And should you still have time to spare after the walk, why not visit the Wildfowl and Wetlands Trust on the other side of the river, almost opposite Burpham.*

## THE WILDFLOWER WALK FROM BURPHAM (1)

Park the car in the Car Park just beyond the George and Dragon in Burpham and cross the recreation ground. After the gate from the children's play area, follow the path directly ahead; this actually crosses the site of an old Saxon fort. Now go down some rather steep steps and cross over the stile. Bear left and keep to the towpath by the River Arun; there are some spectacular views of Arundel Castle from this point. Frequently, grey herons, easily recognizable in flight by their broad slow wing flap, are discreetly stationed amongst the rushes by the river bank. Ducks, coots and moorhens appeared to share this watery stretch in reasonable harmony, whereas half a dozen arrogant swans were constantly at loggerheads with each other.

Continue by the river, crossing a rather complicated footbridge, then turn left into the water-meadows after a further stile. The hedgerows immediately to the left have masses of large juicy blackberries in the autumn and a 'reliable' source tells me the fields are good for mushrooms, especially if they've been grazed by horses. Now cross a stile, turn left and after two more stiles (very close to each other), you'll arrive at a road. Having turned right, ignore the first footpath on the left but take the second. This is after a short bit of road walking and is sited at the top of an incline. A notice indicates the Angmering Park Estates. The bridlepath travels directly through this small but attractive woodland of hazel, beech and oak with a fair bit of blackthorn (sloe) and hawthorn. A flash of green and a 'tap tap' suggested a woodpecker was at work somewhere. Look for jays too; these are one of Britain's most brightly coloured woodland birds, clothed mainly in terracotta and bright blue; curiously, like squirrels, they gather acorns and bury them. The biggest surprise of the walk was seeing the supposedly nocturnal badger lumber unconcernedly across the path ahead ....... it was only 4 p.m. and broad daylight.

Leave the woods by the way of a gate at the end of the track and almost abruptly you'll be on open downland. Keep the line of sparse trees to the left and turn left

# TOUR 9 - FLORA AND FAUNA

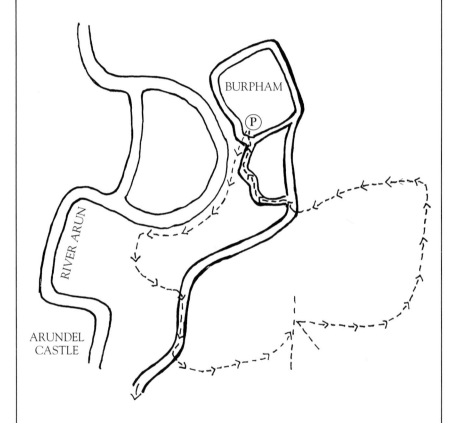

BURPHAM

Ⓟ

RIVER ARUN

ARUNDEL
CASTLE

# THE WILDFLOWER WALK FROM BURPHAM

PUBLIC FOOTPATH – – – –

by a wooden sign, turning right instantly, by another sign. Surrounded by downland, continue to walk northwards along the floor of the valley. Note the tiny chalkhill blue butterflies, prevalent throughout the summer and whose caterpillars feed on the short-stemmed downland flowers such as, horse-shoe vetch. After a gate at the end of the valley, circle to the left and follow the bridlepath uphill. At the top turn left onto a concrete track and carry on past golden cornfields to the bottom of the slope. At the road turn right, then left, back to Burpham.

# WATER-MEADOW FLOWERS:-

**Ladies Smock.**  From March to June the delicate pale pink flowers grow 'en masse' to a height of about twelve inches. Also called 'Milkmaids'.

**Buttercup.**  The simple bright yellow flowers on slender stems can carpet the meadows during the summer.

**Marsh Marigold.**  Similar to a buttercup in appearance except that the leaves are rounded, the stems tougher and it flowers in the spring.

**Willow Herb.**  Up to four foot high, with slender leaves and deep pink flowers, this plant grows abundantly during July and August.

**Watercress.**  Insignificant little white flowers top this perennial aquatic herb, which grows where there is the slightest suggestion of water.

**Meadow Sweet.**  A froth of white flowers with a delicate fragrance on reddish stems, during the summer. Also known as 'Queen of the Meadows'.

**Arum.**  Or 'Lords and Ladies', or 'Cuckoo Pintle'. A tuberous plant with a lot of arrow-shaped leaves, often spotted with black. The greenish white bract leaf unfurls to disclose a deep purple column and the actual flowers are at the base of this. Can also grow in damp woods.

# WOODLAND FLOWERS:-

**Anemone.**  White veined flowers tinged with pink, found from March to June.

**Red Campion.**  Several pink-red flowers on a single rather hairy stem, from June to September.

| | |
|---|---|
| **Honeysuckle.** | Found on the edges of woodland, this perfumed creeper has glorious red berries in the autumn. |
| **Bluebell.** | A familiar sight growing in great carpets of blue beneath the trees, during April and May. |
| **Dog Rose.** | In the summer, the sweet-scented pink flowers and thorny stems often form a climbing plant of six to eight feet high. |
| **Primrose.** | One of the early spring flowers. The pale yellow petals and crinkled leaves can be found in woodland clearings. |
| **Foxglove.** | Growing in the summer months on dry wastes and woodland slopes, foxgloves are probably one of the best loved plants in Britain. The pink hat-shaped flowers usually have speckled insides and droop from the tall stems. |

## DOWNLAND FLOWERS:-

| | |
|---|---|
| **Horse-Shoe Vetch.** | One of the commonest downland plants with vivid yellow flowers on spreading stems, sometimes up to twelve inches long. It can be seen from May until August. |
| **Wild Thyme.** | Deep purple and almost identical to the cultivated variety but generally smaller. It flowers throughout the summer. |
| **Milkwort.** | A delicate ground hugging flower of bluish-purple hue that blooms in June and July. |
| **Orchids.** | The most common varieties on the chalk downs are the 'spotted' and the 'pyramidal' orchids. The spotted has pale pink flowers and dark spots on the leaves. The pyramidal is deep pink. Both flower from June until August. |
| **Scabious.** | A number of lilac coloured flowers borne on slender stems, varying between one foot and three feet high. The flowering period is from June to September. |

| | |
|---|---|
| **Cowslips.** | In the spring, delightfully scented yellow flowers on stoutish stems about six inches high, appear on certain areas of the Downs. |
| **Round-Headed Rampion.** | Unusual deep blue flowers which resemble a cluster of slender bird claws. Only a few inches high with slight stems, Rampion grows during July and August. |
| **Vipers Bugloss.** | Found on all chalky soil or wasteland, this plant appears to thrive on nothing. The summer flowers, first reddish then becoming bright blue, are on prickly stems that can grow to about two foot high. |

## THE WILDFOWL AND WETLANDS TRUST, ARUNDEL (2)

This Trust, first established in Gloucestershire in 1946 by artist and naturalist, the late Sir Peter Scott, is designed to protect our wetlands and their wildlife. Here you will find sixty acres of ponds, lakes and reed beds, all providing a special site for thousands of wild and migratory birds. Discreetly positioned hides offer the chance to see the shyer, more unusual birds at close quarters; others are so tame they'll eat from your hand. There's an excellent visitor centre, a restaurant and a shop. The Wildfowl and Wetlands Trust is open all the year, except for Christmas Day and there is an entrance charge.

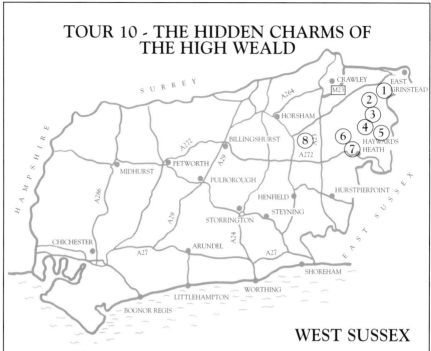

# TOUR 10 - THE HIDDEN CHARMS OF THE HIGH WEALD

## WEST SUSSEX

1. Weir Wood Reservoir
2. The Priest House, West Hoathly
3. Highbrook
4. Horsted Keynes Station and the Bluebell Line
5. Horsted Keynes
6. Ardingly Reservoir
7. Balcombe Viaduct
8. Slaugham

*The Priest House, West Hoathly*

# TOUR 10 - THE HIDDEN CHARMS OF THE HIGH WEALD

*Where and what exactly is the High Weald? The High Weald is an irregular plateau of land, often quite heavily forested and lying between the chalk ranges of the North and South Downs. It begins just east of Horsham and then stretches across the upper regions of Sussex before descending into Kent; the highest point being Crowborough Beacon at 792 feet. The soil is a mix of clay, sand and sandstone, the latter often providing surprising contours in the scenery. The greater part of the High Weald, including Ashdown Forest, is in East Sussex; the wedge-shaped piece in West Sussex is bordered by Horsham, East Grinstead and Haywards Heath. In spite of the proximity of these towns, this outstandingly attractive area of the Weald is remarkably unspoiled; perhaps because it's 'twixt town and coast', and generally tends to be bypassed by the hordes. As this tour illustrates, it's perfectly possible to spend a day discovering the hazy hills, the wildlife and the 'olde-worlde villages', yet hardly see a soul.*

*Whilst meandering along the lanes, you'll probably notice the abundance of lush rhododendrons and azaleas that grow hereabouts. This is due to the rich clay soil which seems to be conducive for growing most plants and makes the district a veritable paradise for magnificent gardens. Five of these gardens, all in natural landscaped settings, are open to the public. However, I have not included them in the tour but simply listed them separately for you to chose the one you would like to add to the day. They all carry an admission charge.*

## WEIR WOOD RESERVOIR (1)

Constructed in 1954 and fed by the River Medway, Weir Wood Reservoir straddles the boundaries of East and West Sussex. Placed in hilly surrounds and overlooked by the unusual Standen Rocks, it has become a bustling metropolis of bird life. Some of the more common birds to look for are: grey herons, mallards, grebes, cormorants and Canada geese. The western end of the reservoir is a nature reserve and on the northern side are several well signed footpaths leading around a part of the lake or up to Standen Rocks. These smooth rocks perch precariously on the hillside looking like unexpected mounds of 'creme caramel'. They form part of the sandstone ridge that runs between Tunbridge Wells and East Grinstead. The sand stones, created form the fossils of plants and invertebrates, are easily eroded by the weather hence their rounded appearance.

A little to the north of the reservoir is Standen House, owned by the National Trust. It was built by the architect, Phillip Webb in 1892 and is a treasury of the work by his friend, the artist and designer, William Morris and will certainly delight the Art Nouveau enthusiast. Standen House and gardens are open from April until the end of October, Wednesday to Sunday, p.m. only. There is an admission charge.

## THE PRIEST HOUSE, WEST HOATHLY (2)

A picturesque Wealden Hall House, sited in one of the most discreet and charming villages in West Sussex. Here, the sense of peaceful isolation is only interrupted by glimpses of the South Downs landscape, seen between the tall beeches and rhododendrons, to remind one there is another world beyond West Hoathly.

It's thought the Priest House was built about 1415 for the Prior of the Cluniac Priory in Lewes, for they owned the West Hoathly estates. Unfortunately the interior no longer follows the traditional Hall House style of being open to the roof (in this case one of mellowed Horsham stone). Instead a floor was inserted during the Elizabethan era, after it had passed into private ownership. Eventually the building was divided into two workman's cottages but by 1900 it had become derelict. In 1905 the property was purchased by a John Godwin King, who converted it into a Folk Museum and opened it to the public in 1908. The house and contents were presented to the Sussex Archeological Society in 1935 and they now open it daily from March until October. Amongst the lovely herbaceous gardens are a hundred and fifty different varieties of herbs, once used in medicine or folklore; the aroma is almost intoxicating.

There is a small entrance charge to visit the Priest House, but do pause before entering and look at the large lump of iron sunk into the threshold: this was supposedly to keep witches from passing through the doorway! West Hoathly lies about four miles south of East Grinstead, on a minor road, off the A22.

## HIGHBROOK (3)

An attractive hamlet positioned on a kind of knoll in this already hilly countryside. Highbrook needs to be visited on a fine day so the far reaching panoramas can be enjoyed to their fullest.

*Horsted Keynes Station*

## HORSTED KEYNES STATION AND THE BLUEBELL LINE (4)

From Highbrook follow the signs southwards to reach Horsted Keynes Railway Station, separated from the village of the same name by more than a mile.

The station, one of the best preserved in the country, is on the Bluebell Line, a nostalgic railway that captures the great age of steam. The historic locomotives and vintage carriages chug through a ten mile stretch of glorious countryside, starting at Sheffield Park and finishing at Kingscote, near East Grinstead. Although the train can be boarded at Horsted Keynes, the headquarters of the Bluebell Railway are at Sheffield Park, where there is a museum and a locomotive collection. For information on train times and charges, phone (01825) 722370/ 723777.

## HORSTED KEYNES (5)

An interesting village with a central green, one or two shops, irregular cottages, a couple of handsome pubs and an old forge, now housing 19th century Indian artifacts; bang on the door of the adjoining cottage for an appointment to view. Do have a look at the Norman church of St. Giles, sited down a narrow lane on the northern side of Horsted Keynes. Buried here is the former Prime Minister, Harold Macmillan, whose home was at the nearby hamlet of Birchgrove.

For a short but pretty walk, continue past the church and follow the path through intermittent woodland until reaching a pleasant expanse of water. This is an old Hammer Pond once used for the production of iron smelting (see 'An Industrial Era').

## ARDINGLY RESERVOIR (6)

Close to the B2026 at Ardingly, this attractively landscaped reservoir offers sailing, fishing, wind surfing and bird-watching facilities. A number of well signed footpaths and bridlepaths give the walker, or the rider, plenty of opportunity to explore the lake's wishbone shaped perimeters. For further information on the range of activities held at the reservoir, contact the Ardingly Activity Centre on (01444) 892549.

## BALCOMBE VIADUCT (7)

A magnificent arched edifice that is best viewed from the minor road between Balcombe village and Haywards Heath, just east of the B2036.

*Ardingly Reservoir*

Built in 1839-1841, this amazing feat of Victorian workmanship has thirty-seven brick arches with each pier being arched at the base, producing an arch within an arch effect. At 1475 feet long, it has to be one of England's most impressive viaducts.

## SLAUGHAM (8)

The picturesque hamlet of Slaugham could have come straight from the pages of a glossy magazine. It's hidden amongst narrow leafy lanes and although close to the busy A23, appears delightfully rural, possibly even isolated. The pocket-sized green is overlooked by a handful of very desirable properties and a pleasant pub. Note the white painted telephone box and no telephone wires; all down to the last Lord of The Manor who was anxious to retain the rustic simplicity of Slaugham.

The church of St. Mary claims to be of Norman origin, with the interior containing several fine brasses and an immense wall tomb. These commemorate the Coverts, a powerful family during the 16th and 17th centuries, whose seat was at Slaugham Place. If you follow the signed footpath through the churchyard, the ruins of the Elizabethan Slaugham Place can easily be seen on the other side of the meadow. The path then continues down to a lake, (yet another hammer pond), which is almost at the source of the Ouse, an East Sussex river.

# GARDENS TO VISIT

## LEONARDSLEE GARDENS, NR. HORSHAM - (01403) 891212

Superb landscaped gardens set in a large valley with magnificent views across several lakes, formerly hammer ponds, (see 'The Industrial Era' for further information). The outstanding variety of brilliant flowers produced by the azaleas and rhododendrons together with other ericaceous species, make Leonardslee a paradise to visit, particularly in the spring. Open from April until October.

## NYMANS GARDENS, HANDCROSS - (01444) 400321

Owned by the National Trust, Nymans contains a superlative collection of rare and beautiful plants from all over the world. Created by the Messel family from 1890 onwards, the walled gardens and sunken gardens are centred around the romantic ruins of the Messels' former home, which was destroyed by fire. Yet somehow the creeper clad shell adds a unique and fascinating aspect to the attraction. Open from April until October.

## BORDE HILL GARDENS, HAYWARDS HEATH - (01444) 450326

Borde Hill is not simply a garden, but two hundred acres of rolling parkland with woods, a lake and an excellent children's area. Beyond a pleasant restaurant is the Victorian walled garden filled with all the herbaceous favourites. On the far side of the main driveway camellias, azaleas and rhododendrons grow in profusion, whilst a 70 foot Chinese tulip tree towers over the Garden of Allah. Open from Easter until October.

## HIGH BEECHES, HANDCROSS - (01444) 400589

Twenty acres of enchanting woodlands and water gardens filled with daffodils, bluebells and other wild flowers are an integral part of High Beeches. A wealth of trees and shrubs, including azaleas and rhododendrons, offer a riot of seasonal colour. Open for six afternoons a week during the spring and autumn.

*Borde Hill Gardens*

## WAKEHURST PLACE, ARDINGLY - (01444) 892701

The Elizabethan house and grounds of Wakehurst Place are managed by the Royal Botanical Gardens at Kew and it is here they store the seeds of many rare and threatened plants. The ornamental gardens, natural woodlands, rocky valleys and picturesque water courses linking several lakes, cover about 170 acres. They contain a rare collection of trees, conifers, shrubs and other plants, as well as providing a conservation area for the flora and fauna of the Sussex Weald. Open throughout the year, except for Christmas Day and New Years Day.

# TOUR 11 - NOT JUST FOR THE GARDENER .....

## WEST SUSSEX

1. West Dean Gardens, West Dean
2. Apuldram Roses, Apuldram Lane, Dell Quay
3. Denmans Gardens, Fontwell, nr Arundel
4. The Dried Flower Barn, Hill Lane, Barnham
5. Roundstone Garden Centre, Angmering
6. Highdown Chalk Gardens, nr Worthing
7. Hollygate Cactus Gardens, Ashington

*Denmans Gardens*

# TOUR 11 - NOT JUST FOR THE GARDENER .....

*What is a gardener? Not somebody who digs the soil and clips hedges for others: nor is it the expert whose only ambition is a First at the Chelsea Flower Show. The Dictionary suggests a gardener is "somebody who cultivates his (or her) own piece of land for personal pleasure." By all accounts, gardening has become one of today's most popular pastimes. This is fairly obvious when visiting a Garden Centre, particularly at the weekend, to see what many of the great British public enjoy doing most with their leisure hours*

*The gardeners of the family will always stand out a mile; for they're the ones who fidget after about ten minutes of sitting and enjoying the results of their horticultural labours. Suddenly a rose need dead-heading; or the tender shoots of Convolvulus will be seen insidiously climbing the Japonica and whilst others continue to laze amongst the Geraniums, the enthusiast will be at work once more. But that, of course, is all a part of the pleasure.*

*With all these things in mind, this tour is planned to be informative for the gardener and enjoyable for any family or friends that come along too. As seeing these attractions can be quite time consuming (and gardeners won't be hurried), I would suggest perhaps visiting only four of the places listed, in any one day.*

## WEST DEAN GARDENS, WEST DEAN (1)

These glorious gardens lie amongst downland near the A286, about six miles north of Chichester. The estate and original Manor House, built during the 17th century, became noted for its rare shrubs and trees and for the last two hundred years has courted eminent horticulturists and Royal visitors, many of whom contributed to the ornamental grounds by planting trees. Today, the knapped flint Manor is now West Dean College, which specializes in courses on the Arts and Crafts. The surrounding thirty-five acres of historic gardens are open daily from March to November and there is an entrance charge.

The restored and walled kitchen garden is particularly interesting, with thirteen glasshouses dating from the 1890's, including peach and fig houses, vineries, an orchid house plus melon and pineapple pits. There's a proper working kitchen garden (just like Grandma's), with vegetables, soft fruits, herbs and flowers. A selection of this mouth-watering produce can be purchased from the shop. Some of the other pleasing features to see at West Dean are a 300 ft Pergola, an Arboretum, a park walk, water gardens, wild gardens and a first class Visitor Centre.

## APULDRAM ROSES, APULDRAM LANE, DELL QUAY (2)

Apuldram is situated between Chichester Harbour and the A286, south of Chichester. A record of the 12th century mentions "Apeldreham Manor", meaning 'homestead with apple trees'. Less than a thousand years later , just such an apple orchard was transformed into Apuldram Rose Garden, an oasis of roses growing in perfumed disarray and resembling an artist's colourfully blended palette. Here, the climbing and rambling roses are entwined with trellises, walls and arbours; you will find Floribundas, Hybrid Teas, Shrubs and Miniatures, some skilfully displayed in terracotta or stone pots. Incorporated into the central part of the garden are beds holding container specimens which are for sale. Close by is a large rose field, where

*Apuldram Roses, Dell Quay*

some three hundred different varieties are grown. Pruning demonstrations, open evenings, a shop with a Rose Information Room and a yearly catalogue are all part of the facilities offered by these specialist rose growers. There is no charge to visit Apuldram which is open all the year except for the Christmas period.

## DENMANS GARDENS, FONTWELL, NEAR ARUNDEL (3)

When Denmans was first purchased in 1945, it was simply a derelict house and farm buildings with thirty-two acres of neglected land. Over the years, a considerable transformation has taken place due to some innovative ideas by the owners, careful planning and a great deal of hard work. The individual technique that has been applied at Denmams is simple and effective. There is a basic structure throughout of evergreens, which are then interwoven with unusual and colourful plants and shrubs. These are then left to self-seed amongst the gravel covering. A walk round Denmams begins in the walled garden, filled with old fashioned favourites, then passes on to the gravel stream and pool, planted with grasses, bamboos and willows. The large sloping south garden has spring bulbs, hellebores and euphorbias, with the trees of Romneya, Magnolia, Japanese Cherry and Acer competing in splendour overhead.

The Clock House is positioned in a separate area and its from here, John Brookes runs a school of landscape design. The courses last for a duration of four weeks and amongst other things, students are taught to recognize a sympathy between design and individual location. There is an admission charge to visit Denmams Gardens which, except for Christmas Day and Boxing Day, is open throughout the year.

## THE DRIED FLOWER BARN, HILL LANE, BARNHAM (4)

Perhaps not quite for the gardener, but nevertheless enjoyable as well as being a useful lesson in seeing just how many different flowers and seed heads can be dried. The selection at the Flower Barn is extensive, as is the range of colours, although my personal choice would be those that are left 'au naturel' and not dyed.

Here's a tip or two for those who want to dry their own flowers. Pick the blooms just before they reach their peak; seed heads as they start to turn colour. Hang in small bunches in a dry place, upside down and out of the sunlight. Sun will cause the flowers to fade and any damp will encourage mildew. In a few weeks you should have some good results. The Dried Flower Barn is open throughout the year and Barnham is sited about three miles south west of the A27 at Arundel.

## ROUNDSTONE GARDEN CENTRE, ANGMERING (5)

This ultimate hypermarket of garden centre is not everybody's 'cup of tea', but if you're searching for something for the garden, you'll surely find it here. The aisles of plants and shrubs appear to stretch for miles, much of it being wheelchair friendly and undercover. There's every conceivable garden accessory from trowels to conservatories; a huge selection of house plants and cut flowers, seeds and bulbs. There are activities for the kids, pets to see, fish in the aquatic department and a mind bending gift section. Oh, and if you're feeling a trifle weary after this lot, there is always Roundstones Coffee Shop on hand to offer a 'pick-me-up'.

Roundstones Garden Centre is open daily all year and is positioned by the A259, three miles east of Littlehampton.

## HIGHDOWN CHALK GARDENS, NEAR WORTHING (6)

Fantastic, famous and free, yet fifty years ago these gardens were nothing more than a worked out chalkpit sited on the downland between Worthing and Littlehampton. It proved to be an irresistible challenge to Sir Frederick and Lady Stern, who lived in the neighbouring 19th century house, Highdown Towers. Both were competent gardeners and they set out to prove that rare and exotic plants would grow in the thin chalky soil and withstand the vagaries of the British weather. Many of the plants had to be imported in seed form from Australia, Africa, America, Europe, China and Tibet. Trying to establish them at Highdown naturally resulted in both successes and failures, although one hardly connects the word 'failure' with this flourishing garden of today. Sir Frederick Stern, a brilliant research biologist, carried out many experiments in his laboratory and the results of his hybridizations are evident in the grounds at Highdown.

Spring and summer at the Chalk Gardens sees a succession of daffodils, snowdrops, anemones, camellias and azaleas, followed by peonies, bearded iris, foxtail lilies, agapanthus and philadelphus. The trees are unusual and provide year round interest; these include a Chinese hornbeam, planted by Queen Mary when she stayed at Highdown Towers in 1937; a Judas tree (from which Judas Iscariot is supposed to have hung himself); this one has particularly deep pink flowers. Indian Horse Chestnuts, Tree Peonies, Birch Bark Cherries, (originally from China), the remains of a Strawberry Tree (due to the hurricane of '87) and Ilex Oaks all contribute to this creative landscape.

In 1967, when Sir Frederick Stern died, Lady Stern followed his wishes and left the entire property to Worthing Borough Council. Highdown Gardens are open all year but note, from the beginning of October until the end of March it's weekdays only. They are situated up a narrow lane which is easy to miss, off the A259, about three and a half miles east of Littlehampton.

## HOLLYGATE CACTUS GARDENS, ASHINGTON (7)

A unique gardens that have been in existence for more than forty years and featured on both the TV and radio. Because of the nature of the plants' requirements, they all have to be in well heated glasshouses. From outside it all looks a bit dilapidated but inside the hothouses lies another world. The extraordinary luscious cacti and succulents, many with brilliant, almost psychedelic flowers, are huge; some reaching to the roof in tropical splendour, others sporting an obscene girth with matching prickles. A number of the cacti are over a hundred and fifty years old and the entire collection consists of more than twenty thousand varieties, many of them originating from Mexico, South America and Africa.

This outstanding attraction is not just for the cactus collector but anybody, as it offers an absorbing insight into a very different aspect of plant life. Hollygate Cactus Gardens has a large sales area and I can almost guarantee you'll want to buy something for that hot sunny window sill. There is stacks of information on how to look after cacti and the staff are very helpful too; a small charge is made for visiting the glasshouse display. The premises are open daily throughout the year and are situated on the B2133 close to the A24 at Ashington.

*Hollygate Cactus Gardens*

# TOUR 12 - FOLLY SPOTTING

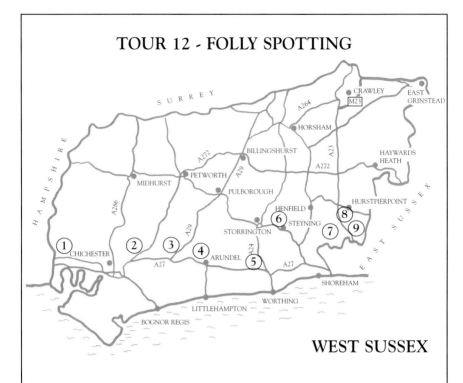

## WEST SUSSEX

1. Racton Tower, nr Aldsworth
2. Halnaker Mill, Halnaker
3. Nore Folly, Slindon
4. Hiorne Tower, Arundel Park
5. High Salvington Windmill,
   High Salvington
6. Wappingthorn Water Tower,
   Steyning
7. The Wellhouse, Fulking
8. Clayton Tunnel, Clayton
9. Jack and Jill Windmills, Clayton

*Hiorne Tower, Arundel Park*

# TOUR 12 - FOLLY SPOTTING

*Is a folly simply an extravagant and useless structure? Or is it a strangely shaped building rendered useless by progress, yet fortunately preserved for posterity. Perhaps only the beholder can decide. I do know however, that when researching the rather nebulous history of these so-called follies, most initially had a use, albeit only for pleasure. Some follies started life as the estate shooting lodge, although frequently, underlying indications suggested the Lord of the Manor would commandeer it for privately entertaining his mistress! There were the tales of the towers being used as 'look-outs' for signalling the 'all clear' to the smuggling fraternity. Other oddly styled buildings had more of an industrial purpose, such as windmills or water towers. Possibly it's a bit misleading to refer to the two latter as follies, but windmills in particular, are unusual structures and as they play such an important part of the Sussex landscape, it would be a shame to miss them.*

*The Folly Spotting tour stretches across the entire breadth of West Sussex, from border to border and follows an almost horizontal line. All except two of the follies are visible from the road and half have a short walk to reach them. Come rain or come shine, it makes an interesting and fun day out.*

## RACTON TOWER, NEAR ALDSWORTH (1)

Facing southwards against a tree covered hill, Racton Tower bears a marked resemblance to a ruinous portion of a castle. Triangular in shape, with three small outer towers and a tall central one, the folly was built by Theodosius Keene for the third Earl of Halifax, who lived at Stansted Park. Erected during the latter part of the 18th century, it cost in excess of £10,000, but fulfilled the purpose of keeping the local inhabitants employed during particularly hard times. As to its use thereafter - the tales grow with the telling.

Apparently, Lord Halifax had a fetish for firing guns from the top of the tower at any time of the day or night. Legend also suggests he would invite the Excise men to Racton, plying them with enough booze to befuddle their wits and enable the smugglers to pass by undetected. Due to its commanding position, this peculiar folly was supposed to play a part in the Napoleonic Wars by acting as a beacon for ships coming into Chichester Harbour.

Racton Tower is sited at the top of a short bridlepath just south of Lordington on the B2146 from Funtingdon, west of Chichester. Should you not fancy the ten minute stroll, then take the minor road to Aldsworth and from there you will obtain an excellent view of the folly across a couple of fields.

## HALNAKER MILL, HALNAKER (2)

Beautifully preserved, the shell of this attractive tower mill can be seen standing high on the downland overlooking Halnaker, Goodwood and Chichester. Built around 1750 for the Goodwood estate, it has been restored twice; first in 1934 by Sir William Bird of Eastham in memory of his late wife and then again in the 1950's by the County Council. The external features of this mill are particularly pleasing; hung with warm terracotta tiles and crowned by a white beehive cap and graceful

*Halnaker Mill*

sweeps, it claims to be one of the oldest windmills in Sussex. Although there is no internal machinery, it's well worth the glorious thirty minute walk to visit Halnaker Mill, which is free and open at all times. To get there, take the signed path through Warehead Farm, just after Halnaker, on the A285 north east of Chichester.

## NORE FOLLY, SLINDON (3)

Owned by the National Trust, the 18th century Nore Folly lies in the grounds of the Slindon Estate. Supposedly, the arched facade was based on a similar Italian building and this is mainly what is still standing today; there's only scant evidence of the thatched summerhouse that once lay behind and was used as a shooting lodge.

To find Nore Folly, take the road to Slindon from the A27 at Fontwell, about four miles west of Arundel. Follow the road through the village and immediately after Slindon College, turn right down a lane and you'll see the folly on rising ground to the left. There is a bridlepath by Courthill Farm leading to Nore Folly and it will take about fifteen minutes to get there. Do explore Slindon whilst you're here. The village is almost totally unspoilt and there are some fine examples of brick and flint houses and extremely pretty gardens.

## HIORNE TOWER, ARUNDEL PARK (4)

For a folly, the triangular Hiorne Tower appears almost perfect, as it stands splendidly situated, in the 1000 acre Arundel Park, fairly close to the entrance north of Arundel Castle. This Gothic building with chequered stonework was erected by the architect, Frances Hiorne in the late 18th century, for the Duke of Norfolk, presumably as a hunting lodge. The style of architecture is reminiscent of the Castle itself and for a short time it was supposedly occupied. The park, which is noted for its many beautiful walks and magnificent trees, has unrestricted public access on foot, but neither dogs, nor cars are allowed.

## HIGH SALVINGTON WINDMILL, HIGH SALVINGTON (5)

Once it stood amongst fields, now High Salvington Windmill stands amongst suburbia about half a mile north of the A27 at Worthing. It's indicated from the A24, leading to Findon. This black Post Mill was constructed between 1700 and 1720 and ceased milling in 1897. Restoration work on the derelict building began in 1976 and now, with most of the machinery installed, it's more or less in full working order for milling flour once more. Opening times are from April to September on the first and third Sunday of each month, p.m. only. A road passes the mill, so you can always obtain an excellent view of it.

## WAPPINGTHORN WATER TOWER, STEYNING (6)

A curiously designed pagoda-type water tower, built at the beginning of the 20th century. An uncovered stairway winds round the outside giving access to the gazebo perched at the top; the rest of the tower is full of water. The folly is not really visible from the road but can be approached via a footpath or a track passing Wappingthorn Farm. Both of these are off the B2135, just north of Steyning.

# THE WELLHOUSE, FULKING (7)

The charming village of Fulking has been associated with sheep rearing for the last five hundred years; therefore, it's hardly surprising the very popular pub is called The Shepherd and Dog. When approaching the village from the west, it sits in an

*The Wellhouse, Fulking*

elevated position on a sharp corner (you can't miss it), with the Fulking Springs burbling away in the foreground. Adjacent to the springs is the tiny Victorian Gothic Wellhouse with a tiled plaque on one side saying-:

"He sendeth springs into the valleys which run amongst the hills.

Oh, that men would praise the Lord for his goodness."

In years past the springs used to be dammed in the hollow of the lane, just below the pub, to provide a sheep wash.

Round the corner from the Shepherd and Dog is yet another 'water related' folly. This time it's a red brick fountain; a memorial to John Rushkin, the art critic who was instrumental in obtaining a permanent water supply to the village.

# CLAYTON TUNNEL, CLAYTON (8)

Before turning southwards onto the A273, stop for a minute to see an example of the Victorians' love of extravagantly useless architecture, which in this case extended to railway tunnels. The ornate castellated entrance heralds the tunnel on the main London - Brighton rail route. It burrows under the Downs at Clayton, to reappear at a relatively simple entrance on the southern side. It was officially opened in 1841 and the twin turrets, arrowslits and battlements make it appear like a Disney Castle. In later years the space between the turrets provided an extraordinary site for building a cottage. Surely, it must be like living on top of a constantly rumbling earthquake!

# JACK AND JILL WINDMILLS, CLAYTON -(9)

Placed on the apex of the Downs and silhouetted against the skyline are the husband and wife pair of windmills, Jack and Jill. Jack is a black Tower Mill, built on site in 1866 and worked until 1906. Jill is a white Post Mill, built in Brighton about 1821 and with the assistance of eighty oxen, moved to her present site in 1852. Like her husband she ceased milling in 1906.

To reach the windmills, follow the A273 southwards and about half a mile after Clayton, take the lane to the east. This leads right up to the windmills where there is ample parking, superb views and some scenic walks across the Downs. Jill, the white Post Mill, is open on Sunday afternoons during the season. Jack is now in private ownership and not open to the public.

*'Jill', a white Post Mill at Clayton*

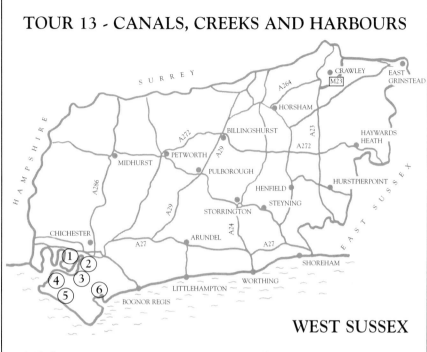

# TOUR 13 - CANALS, CREEKS AND HARBOURS

**WEST SUSSEX**

1. Bosham
2. Dell Quay
3. Birdham and The Chichester Canal
4. West Itchenor
5. The Witterings
6. Sidlesham Quay and Pagham Harbour

*Bosham*

# TOUR 13 - CANALS, CREEKS AND HARBOURS

*The spire of Chichester Cathedral and the opulent grandstand of Goodwood Racecourse are the occasional and distant landmarks from this flat coastal elbow of West Sussex. Here, the narrow roads twist and turn between high hedgerows, then suddenly ending, give way to fishermen's cottages, quayside pubs and all manner of sailing boats, moored in yet another of Chichester Harbour's hidden creeks.*

*Most of the West Sussex coastline has little to commend it, being overdeveloped and overcrowded. The landscape south of Chichester appears to have escaped this fate providing instead, a haven for the yachtsman, a fertile plain for the farmer and an area that is rich with marine history and ecology for the visitor to explore.*

## BOSHAM (1)

Nestling in unspoilt surroundings about four miles west of Chichester is the quaint village of Bosham (pronounced Bozzum). Steeped in history, its lingering charm captivates every writer and artist, not to mention the yachtsman who sails discreetly up the narrow channel.

During Roman times Bosham became an important port being close to the Palace at Fishbourne (see Roman Sussex). The Holy Trinity Church, which is of Saxon origin, was built on the foundations of a Roman basilica. In AD 681, St. Wilfred of York found Christianity was being preached by Dicul, an Irish monk, and his five brethren, supposedly from the tiny crypt that can still be seen beneath the church. In the 11th century King Canute is reputed to have had some sort of local royal residence and the theory that his little daughter was buried here, has been supported by the evidence of an exhumation in 1865 of a Saxon coffin bearing the remains of an eight year old child. Legend goes on to suggest it was from here that Canute rebuked the waves! Bosham is also depicted on the Bayeux Tapestry, woven shortly after the Conquest of 1066. It shows King Harold entering the Holy Trinity, prior to sailing to Normandy to meet William.

Today Bosham appears like an irresistible dream on the horizon waiting to be discovered. But before you park your car on the waterfront road and hasten off, pause and read the little notice on the wall; it says "This road is covered at each high tide". There is plenty to see and it's not meant to be hurried over. A visit to the historic church is a must; then a walk along Quay Meadow, where the tarred sheds on the quay itself are known as The Raptackle and once housed rope and gear for shipping: the nearby watermill is now the headquarters of the local sailing club. There is a very good gallery and craft centre where you can also have coffee and afterwards a wander down the picturesque High Street will bring you to a waterside inn, "The Anchor Bleu".

Do take a short ride southwards to Bosham Hoe. Apart from being pretty, you will get a chance to see the much photographed view of Bosham, taken from the other side of the creek.

## DELL QUAY (2)

Impossible to believe that the diminutive and charming harbour of Dell Quay was once the main medieval port for Chichester. Built during the latter part of the 14th century by the Lord Fitzwilliams of Cowdray, it rose to great heights of prosperity during Tudor times; thereafter, the port was troubled by constant silting up which prevented the larger boats and their shipments from landing. In spite of this, a flourishing trade in grain continued until the 18th century. Small vessels, which were still able to use the harbour, contained cargoes of produce, fish, leather, wood and stone. Imports included barges carrying coal from Sunderland. In later years the Quay was leased to merchants dealing in cattle fodder and their last shipment was unloaded in the 1930's.

The long views directly up the channel to Chichester and the Downs probably haven't changed that much. But instead of being a working port it is now used entirely for pleasure and is filled with the gracefully slender sailing craft of today's enthusiasts. The old warehouses are the headquarters of the Dell Quay Sailing Club and William Tipper's 17th century mill has been severely truncated and incorporated in Dell Quay House. This little harbour lies about two miles from Chichester, just off the A286.

*A creek, near Dell Quay*

## BIRDHAM AND THE CHICHESTER CANAL (3)

Birdham sprawls around the A286, some four miles south west of Chichester: over the years it has become increasingly popular with the sailing fraternity and the little road that leaves Birdham to the north leads to two of the biggest marinas in Chichester Harbour. The first, Birdham Pool, was constructed from a part of an old mill pond and the unusual tide mill buildings are still there today. The second marina, Chichester Yacht Basin, now offers extensive facilities for both yachts and cruisers. Alongside the basin is Salterns Locks; still operating, it controls the western end of the Chichester Canal and the former lock keeper's cottage is part of the Chichester Yacht Club's premises.

Chichester Canal once formed a section of the Portsmouth/Arundel Canal route, built to connect with other inland waterways leading from Portsmouth to London. It was formally opened on April 19th 1822. It was designed to accommodate vessels of up to a hundred tons and its main object was to overcome the necessity of transferring cargoes from large to small boats at Itchenor, then into wagons at Dell Quay before finally reaching Chichester. However, it was not the commercial success it should have been, due amongst other things, to the railways becoming more efficient. By 1892 the Portsmouth and Arundel Navigation Company had closed down and the canal was taken over by the Corporation of Chichester. They in turn, abandoned it in 1928 and it was eventually purchased by the West Sussex County Council in 1957.

Today, this important area of our industrial heritage is in the care of the Chichester Canal Society, a registered charity whose aims are to restore, develop and improve the entire canal as a leisure amenity for the public. The Society also provides an excellent booklet on its history, the canal walks, their relative points of interest and the wildlife. The booklet can be purchased from the Tourist Information Office in Chichester.

## WEST ITCHENOR (4)

The road at West Itchenor sweeps abruptly down to this harbourside village and one is suddenly confronted by a watery expanse filled with a bevy of sailing boats. Even the houses perpetuate the nautical scenery by having a boat, or some sort of sailing gear, filling the front gardens and the local pub is appropriately called "The Ship". From here a ferry operates, crossing the channel to Bosham Hoe. At the Harbour Office, which is open on weekdays throughout the year, visitors can obtain information about the service and also about the history of the harbour in general.

Adjacent to the Harbour Office, but nothing to do with it, are Wingate Water Tours. This company organizes boat trips that explore the mouth of Chichester Harbour. The trips last about an hour and a half and it really is a pleasure to see so much of this unspoilt area from the water. For those interested, either call at the office or telephone (01243) 786418. A word of advice - take lots of warm sweaters.

Follow the A286 from Chichester; this will become the B2179 and Itchenor will be signed to the right.

## THE WITTERINGS (5)

The coastal villages of East and West Wittering have a mile between them and the Tudor Cakeham Tower, the only surviving relic of the Bishops of Chichester Palace, which is now incorporated with Cakeham Manor. West Wittering is the smaller of the two and has an interesting church and a reasonably attractive village centre. East Wittering is different altogether, being much more developed with shops, restaurants and guest houses. In a way it's reminiscent of childhood holidays;

*Sidlesham Quay*

*Pagham Harbour*

deserted beaches due to suddenly chilly weather, steamed up cafes and those plastic windmill things on a stick that whizz round in the wind. This is really a bucket and spade holiday place, for the beaches which stretch for some miles are, at low tide, gloriously sandy. The kids would love it, providing the weather stays fine. The Witterings are situated on the coast, south of Chichester on the B2179.

## SIDLESHAM QUAY AND PAGHAM HARBOUR (6)

Centrally placed to Pagham Harbour, Sidlesham Quay consists of a few picturesque cottages, a farm or two and The Crab and Lobster Inn. Until 1900 a tide mill stood on the grassy frontage, the nearby mill pond being filled with the rising tide; as the sea receded the water then operated the mill machinery. Records suggest that Sidlesham Quay has been used as some sort of harbour since Saxon times. But it was not until the Middle Ages, or later, that it became a port of any consequence, the mill indicating a trade in grain. By the 1870's, seafaring business had declined and the harbour was then reclaimed for agriculture by damming the mouth with shingle banks. In 1910 the sea broke through this barrier and since then the coastal scenery has looked much as you see today.

Pagham Harbour and the surrounding countryside has now become a Nature Reserve managed by the West Sussex County Council. It is a site of exceptional interest to the bird watcher, naturalist or walker and the entire area covers about 653 hectares, the harbour salt marsh being about 283 hectares of that amount. A public footpath follows the perimeter of the harbour, finishing at Pagham on one side and Church Norton on the other. This path also passes the Visitor Centre, situated just south of Sidlesham on the Selsey road. Here you can obtain all sorts of information about the Nature Reserve and its associated flora and fauna, plus a programme of events, including guided walks throughout the year.

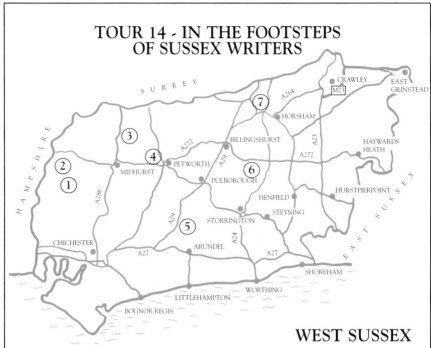

# TOUR 14 - IN THE FOOTSTEPS
## OF SUSSEX WRITERS

## WEST SUSSEX

1. H.G. Wells, Uppark, nr South Harting
2. Anthony Trollope, North End, South Harting
3. Lord Alfred Tennyson, Aldworth House, Blackdown
4. Wilfred Scawen Blunt, Petworth House, Petworth
5. John Galsworthy, Bury House, Bury
6. Hilaire Belloc, Kings Land and Shipley Mill, Shipley
7. Percy Bysshe Shelley, Field Place, Warnham

*The Causeway, Horsham*

# TOUR 14 - IN THE FOOTSTEPS OF SUSSEX WRITERS

*The number of writers (and artists), who have found Sussex a haven for inspiration is endless. The haunting atmosphere and the gentle beauty of the Downs, the Weald and the sea, has captured their imagination, often giving rise to great waves of nostalgia when absent for any length of time. That famous Sussex author, Hilaire Belloc, whose account of his walks across the Downs, together with his favourite watering places were immortalized in 'The Four Men', writes thus:-*

> *"If I ever become a rich man*
> *Or if I ever grow to be old,*
> *I will build a house with a deep thatch*
> *To shelter me from the cold.*
> *And there shall the Sussex songs be sung*
> *And the story of Sussex told."*

*To follow the footsteps of any writer, will always be a path of illuminating discovery. It could be likened to peeping through the door into a prolific garden of words and seeing it through the eyes of the creator for the first time.*

*So come with me, let's take the scenic route across the Downs above South Harting and find out a little more about those eminent authors and the impression (if any) Sussex made on their lives. Just two things to remember before you set off: firstly, make an early start, as the tour is fairly lengthy: secondly, choose a fine clear day because the panoramas are stunning, particularly from Lord Tennyson's old house at Blackdown, where he wrote:-*

> *"You came and looked and loved the view*
> *Long known and loved by me,*
> *Green Sussex fading into blue*
> *With one grey glimpse of sea."*

## H. G. WELLS (1866 - 1946)
## UPPARK, NR. SOUTH HARTING (1)

Uppark, elegant once more, has risen like a god from the ashes to emulate its former splendour in every minute detail. The classical 17th century facade is no longer blackened and faceless from the fire that ravaged the interior one August day in 1989. The restoration work, using skilled craftsmen and modern techniques, was remarkable and by 1995, Uppark had been opened to the public once again.

Herbert George Wells, the distinguished novelist, spent his formative years at Uppark where his mother, who had been born in Midhurst, was housekeeper to Miss Fetherstonhaugh. He was fortunate in being allowed to use the library at Uppark so he could indulge in his passion for reading. He also explored the Harting Downs and the little villages, in particular Midhurst, which he adored.

"I know of no other county that compares with West Sussex", he later wrote.

His book 'The Wheels of Chance', has the main character cycling through the Sussex villages during the 1890's. HGW was educated at the Grammar School in Midhurst and when he was fifteen worked in a nearby chemist's shop as an apprentice. Although he did not follow this career, the experience was used in

'Tono Bungay'. Two years later he was back in Midhurst again as a pupil teacher at the Grammar School. He lodged next door to the Angel Hotel and draws on this part of his life in 'Love and Mr. Lewisham'.

H.G.Wells was a writer of both fiction and non-fiction. His books were and still are, well read and some have been adapted for radio and television. Uppark, his boyhood abode, is situated on a beautiful stretch of Harting Downs, one and a half miles south of South Harting on the B2146. It's open to visitors from the beginning of April until the end of October. For opening times and admission charges telephone (01730) 825857.

## ANTHONY TROLLOPE (1815 - 1881)
## NORTH END, SOUTH HARTING (2)

The copper clad spire of the church in South Harting provides a startling bright green landmark, nestling at the foot of the Downs. There is a marvellous view of it as one descends from Uppark. In the churchyard there is a curious War Memorial by Eric Gill, a Sussex engraver, stone carver and typographer. The village is the largest of the three Hartings, (the others being East and West) and its all mellow brick cottages, climbing roses and a couple of good looking inns.

*South Harting, home of Trollope*

The 19th century novelist, Anthony Trollope moved to South Harting just two years before his death, in the hopes that the soft downland air would cure his worsening asthma. In spite of his illness, he still followed his aggressive regime for writing; this was to rise at 5.30 a.m. and write two hundred and fifty words every fifteen minutes, only stopping when two and a half thousand had been completed.

He scoffed at the idea of ever needing any environmental inspirations, so perhaps this explains his prolific lifelong output. Initially, his work was not that popular, but when the famous Barchester series were produced, he found almost instant success.

Sadly, the downland air failed to provide him with a magical cure, although he still managed to complete four more novels in that final two years at South Harting. This included 'An Old Man's Love'.

## LORD ALFRED TENNYSON (1809 - 1892)
## ALDWORTH HOUSE, BLACKDOWN (3)

The drive from South Harting to Blackdown is even lovelier if you initially take the slightly longer route following the Downs eastwards. This passes through the delightful farming villages of East Harting, Elsted, Treyford and Didling. Do stop for a minute at Didling and visit St. Andrews Church, which is quite detached from its hamlet. Of Saxon origin and known as the 'Shepherds Church', it's tiny, simple and very charming. The road continues on through Bepton and at Cocking joins the A286 to Midhurst (H.G.Wells favourite place). From Midhurst take the A272 towards Petworth, turning northwards to Lodsworth after a short distance. Blackdown is now about four miles and you can't miss it; a massive hill which at 919 feet is higher than any of the South Downs. It lies close to the Hampshire border and the dark, rather forbidding appearance is due to the covering acres of heather and holly.

Born in Lincolnshire, Lord Alfred Tennyson was appointed Poet Laureate in 1850 and moved to a remote part of Blackdown in 1868. He hoped that by building his 'Temple of the Winds' high above Lurgashall, he would find the privacy and solitude he was seeking. He obviously did, for Aldworth House remained his home until his death in 1892.

Aldworth is now in private ownership and not open to visitors but it can be approached via a public footpath. Do explore Lurgashall, it's the epitome of an English village; beamed cottages, a pub and the church where Tennyson worshipped on Sunday mornings are traditionally set around an attractive village green.

## WILFRED SCAWEN BLUNT (1840 - 1922)
## PETWORTH HOUSE, PETWORTH (4)

Wilfred Blunt, diplomat, poet and writer whose literary publications, including his diaries, frequently aroused a great deal of controversy. Something of a rebel, he travelled extensively in Europe, India and the Middle East, often getting involved with their politics. His spells in West Sussex were rather fragmented, although he was one of the few writers to actually be born in the county.

Blunt entered the world in grand style at the magnificent Petworth House in Petworth Park, where his aunt and cousins were living. The first part of his childhood was spent in Petworth then his mother, who by then had become a widow, took her children to France. Having left school, Blunt entered the diplomatic service and in his mid twenties, inherited the family estate near Crawley in Sussex. He married Byron's granddaughter, Lady Annabel Noel and together they explored the Middle East, finally returning to Crabbet Park to remodel the house and breed Arab horses. The marriage didn't last due to Blunt's constant infidelities and after their separation his wife remained living at Crabbet Park and he moved to Newbuildings Place near Dragons Green.

Out of all his houses only Petworth House, now owned by the National Trust, is open to the public. This is daily (except Thursdays and Fridays) from the beginning of April until the end of October and there is an admission charge.

## JOHN GALSWORTHY (1867 - 1933)
## BURY HOUSE, BURY (5)

John Galsworthy, novelist and dramatist chose to spend the last seven years of his life in the enchanting village of Bury, playing the country gentleman he so often depicted in his novels. He is probably best remembered for 'The Forsyte Saga', the well known series dealing with a family of landed gentry and their social conflicts with the modern world. Many of his books and plays appeared to follow this theme. His own life conformed to that of a well born Englishman; schooling at Harrow then on to Oxford, afterwards gaining worldly experience by travelling. His first novel was published when he was thirty-one, with his first play being produced shortly after. He subsequently went on to write about thirty books as well as a number of plays.

Galsworthy has been described as a modest and likeable man and in 1932 had the great honour of being awarded the Nobel Prize for Literature. A plaque on the front of Bury House commemorates his time in the village. Bury, which is prettily situated on sloping ground leading down to the River Arun, is located near the A29, Arundel to Pulborough road.

## HILAIRE BELLOC (1870 - 1953)
## KINGS LAND AND SHIPLEY MILL, SHIPLEY (6)

As we weave through the chequerwork of fields from Bury, a glimpse of the galleried windmill at Shipley appears through the trees; the approach hasn't really altered since Belloc chanced upon it in 1905. How the ancient little village of Shipley must have appealed to his love of history. There is evidence here of Roman and Saxon occupation; a few fragments of the Norman Knepp Castle still stand and the charming 12th century church once had a large Templar monastery adjoining it.

Hilaire Belloc, historian, author, politician, poet and complex character, whose prolific writings were often associated with Sussex, the county he loved best. He was born at St. Cloud near Paris and Madame Belloc, his mother who was of Anglo-Irish descent, moved to Slindon in Sussex after the death of her French husband. Hilaire was about two at the time. When he was ten he went to The Oratory and then to Oxford, where he won a first in History. After a stint in the French Army, he married an Irish-American girl, Elodie Hogan.

By 1905 he and Elodie had returned to live in Sussex and that same year discovered Kings Land at Shipley. In 1906 they purchased the house, which was then the village shop, together with an adjacent cottage, a windmill and five acres of land. It cost

£900. By this time Belloc was already an accomplished author and inveterate traveller. His walk across France to Switzerland and on to Italy, had resulted in the successful 'Path to Rome'. He had written biographies on both Robespierre and Danton; for children he penned the 'Bad Child's Book of Beasts'; later came 'Cautionary Tales'. His book 'The Four Men' tells of a sailor, an old man, a poet and "myself", walking across Sussex. For a few years he sat in the House of Commons as a Liberal, then resigned, disenchanted with the general political caboodle. He was an inexhaustible writer and at the time of his death (almost forty years after Elodie) he'd had around 150 titles published, plus never ending articles and poetry.

*Belloc's 'Shipley Mill'*

Kings Land is not open to the public, but Shipley Windmill has been restored as a memorial to Hilaire Belloc. It's in full working order and is open to visitors on the first and third Sunday of each month, p.m. only, from April until October. Shipley is situated just off the A272, about four miles east of Billingshurst.

## PERCY BYSSHE SHELLEY (1792 - 1822)
## FIELD PLACE, WARNHAM (7)

No doubt the lanes of Warnham were a great deal more rural when Shelley was born at his ancestral home, Field Place, a Georgian mansion near Warnham. In spite of his boyhood life of wealth and comfort, Percy Bysshe Shelley was not particularly happy at home. He did however, enjoy exploring the countryside surrounding Horsham together with his five sisters and younger brother. He went to school at Eton and then to Oxford, where he was expelled for his unorthodox views. By the age of nineteen he had written 'Queen Mab' and with his subsequent 'Adonais', came to be regarded as the most brilliant poetic genius of the 19th century. He married Harriet Westbrook whilst still very young and during the next six years toured throughout England, Ireland and Europe. He then proceeded to form some complicated liaisons, including one with a Mary Godwin, whom he eventually married after Harriet committed suicide. In 1818 the couple left England to spend time with friends, including Byron, abroad. It was on July 8th in 1822 that the boat Shelley was sailing in capsized in a storm and tragically he was drowned. He was twenty-nine.

Probably there is not really much to remind one of Shelley at Warnham, although the village and the church of St. Margaret make a pleasant place to visit with buildings dating from the 17th century onwards. Field Place is set deep amongst the trees and is not open to the public. But Horsham Museum in the Causeway, Horsham devotes an entire area to the life and works of Percy Bysshe Shelley. It's certainly something the enthusiast should not miss and admission to the museum is free.

*The Shelley Corner in Horsham Museum*

# TOUR 15 - A WALK AROUND CHICHESTER

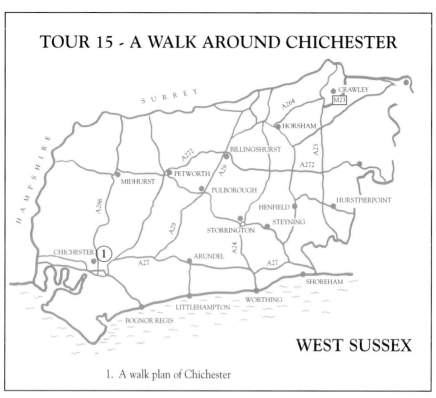

**WEST SUSSEX**

1. A walk plan of Chichester

*Pallant House, Chichester*

# TOUR 15 - A WALK AROUND CHICHESTER

*Chichester, a compact and interesting little city dominated by a magnificent Norman cathedral. This is a city whose Roman ramparts harbour two thousand years of history and a city where yesterday meets today in a timeless union. It proves to be an irresistible attraction for the visitor who feels compelled to explore its ancient precincts. So why not discover Chichester by leaving the car in one of the many Car Parks and making your way to the old Market Cross. Now follow the walk plan and let your footsteps take you around the town first planned by the Romans; subsequently occupied by the Saxons; the subject of great building works by the Normans only to be, after a period of relative calm, despoiled by the Civil War of 1642. Happily a great deal of reconstruction work took place during the Georgian era, leaving posterity some wonderful examples of this sympathetic architecture. The present name dates from the Saxon conquest of 477 AD. and is derived from "Cissas Ceaster" or, fortified town: Cissas being the son of Aella, the Saxon leader. The Romans had previously called it "Noviomagus" (see Roman Sussex for further information). After the Norman Conquest in 1066, Chichester's feudal Lord was Roger de Montgomery, founder of Arundel Castle. The building of Chichester Cathedral took place during the end of the 11th century, under the jurisdiction of Bishop Ralph de Lutta. However, although there was a dedication in 1108, for various reasons including fire, it was not actually consecrated until 1184.*

*Historically, Chichester's economy has been based on commerce. Its position amidst fertile plains has ensured an excellent trade in agriculture and the relatively easy access to Chichester Harbour meant a thriving business in both the importing and exporting of goods. During medieval times the city was also a centre for the wool trade. Small wonder that over the years wealthy merchants and farmers made their homes here; Pallant House, which is open to the public, is just one opulent example.*

*So what of Chichester today? Has its past provided the present with a new industry called 'tourism'? Probably, for first and foremost the beautiful Cathedral undoubtedly attracts thousands of visitors. But, albeit somewhat altered, Chichester still continues to feel like a Market Town: true, there are no longer sheep penned and for sale in East Street, nor do street vendors surround the Market Cross. The Trader's Hall that once stood in North Street had been demolished by the mid 18th century and the old Butter Market now houses a discrete shopping arcade. Today the main thoroughfare is thankfully pedestrianized and always appears to be busy. Shops have their wares tastefully displayed so as not to offend their Georgian facades and intimate little restaurants offer tempting fare; even the Antique Centres appear sufficiently disorderly to look inviting. And what's more, there is still a large twice weekly market, selling anything and everything. It's held on Wednesdays and Saturdays on the site of the former cattle market, just outside the City wall.*

*The Market Cross, Chichester*

# TOUR 15 - A WALK AROUND CHICHESTER

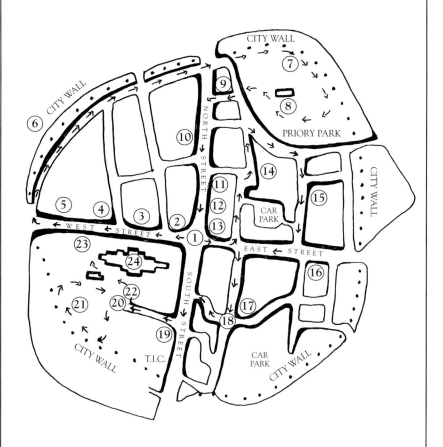

# CHICHESTER, CITY CENTRE WALK PLAN

# WALK PLAN

1.  **The Market Cross.** Erected in 1501 by Bishop Storey, this elaborate cross gave the poor people of Chichester the right to sell their goods 'honestly and fairly'. This they did for the next three hundred years.

2.  **The Dolphin and Anchor.** Situated in West Street, opposite the Cathedral, these two rival coaching inns amalgamated in 1910 to become one establishment. The building is 18th and early 19th century.

3.  **The Army and Navy.** A well known department store now occupies the former Oliver Whitby School for boys, founded in 1702. The school, which closed in 1950, became famous for its uniform of 'Blue Coats'. Look for the Oliver Whitby crest, which is still above the main entrance.

4.  **St. Peter's Church.** Built in 1852, this lovely church is, rather sadly, no longer in use as a place of worship. Instead, it has been converted to accommodate an arcade of shops which give the interior the impression of being rather forlorn.

5.  **Wren House.** Although of the Wren style, this handsome town house was not actually designed by that eminent architect. Constructed in 1696 for a wealthy malster, it has recently undergone much restoration work by the West Sussex County Council, who have owned the property for a number of years.

6.  **The City Wall.** The Romans fortified Chichester around the 2nd century A.D. The original city wall was probably of earth, later to rebuilt in flint. The entirety surrounds about a hundred acres and is approximately 1 1/2 miles in length. Although the main gateways have gone, the rest have been beautifully preserved over the years. It's still perfectly possible to walk right round the walls and the Tourist Information Centre has a good leaflet headed 'City Walls Walk', which gives a very adequate history and a guide.

7.  **Chichester Castle.** All that remains of this 11th century Motte and Bailey type castle is a mound in the corner of the rather pleasant Priory Park.

8.  **The Guildhall.** Also in Priory park is the Guildhall. This is simply the chancel of the church that belonged to the 13th century monastery of the Grey Friars. It is now used as a museum and is open on Saturdays from June to September.

9.  **Ship Hotel.** On the corner of Guildhall Street and North Street is the Ship Hotel, originally erected around 1790 as a private house for one of Nelson's Admirals, Sir George Murray.

10. **31, North Street.** This lovely 18th century property is now the business premises of the Wine and Spirit Merchant, Arthur Purchase. Note the rather fine cantilevered first floor window.

11. **Council Chambers.** A handsome porticoed building, erected for the city in 1731 and then had the rear Assembly Rooms added in 1783. Displayed just inside the ground floor archways is the famous Neptune and Minerva Stone, which documents the dedication of a Roman Temple. (See Roman Sussex).

12. **St. Olaves.** An attractive little church of Saxon origin, which now appears to be rather overcrowded by its neighbouring buildings.

13. **Market House.** Also known as the Butter Market this property, built by Nash in 1807 superseded the Market Cross. Shortly after its erection, a local law was passed indicating that all stall holders selling produce, must do so from the Butter Market and not on the streets.

14. **St. Mary's Hospital.** The delightful St. Martin's Street and St. Martin's Square lead northwards from East Street, just after the Market Cross. Tucked into the corner of St. Martin's Square is the long, low building of St. Mary's Hospital. First established in the latter half of the 13th century, St. Mary's is no longer a working hospital, but has instead been converted into Almshouses. It is perfectly possible to visit the former hospital and see one of the conversions. The opening times are usually in the afternoon, but do check with the Tourist Information Centre first.

15. **City Museum.** Situated in one of Chichester's quiet streets, bearing the unlikely name of Little London, is the District Museum. Housed in an 18th century converted Corn Mill, it offers two floors of excellent displays and information on life in the area since Roman times. It's open from Tuesday to Saturday throughout the year and there is no admission charge.

16. **The Corn Exchange.** An impressive colonnaded building erected in 1830 and used for holding corn auctions. Since the auctions ceased it has been both a theatre and a cinema, the latter closing in the 1980's. At the moment it is being used as a restaurant.

17. **Pallant House.** An enviable blend of Queen Anne and Georgian architecture make up the 'former' home of Chichester's prosperous wine merchant, Henry Peckham. Built for him in 1712, it cost somewhere in the region of three thousand pounds. Pallant House, also known as Dodo House, because of the stone birds by the entrance, is open to the public throughout the year from Tuesday to Saturday. It contains a fine collection of paintings, works of art and interestingly, each room is designed to reflect the history of the house itself.

18. **The Pallants.** Four streets, respectively North, South, East and West Pallant make up The Pallants. These contain some of the loveliest examples of Chichester's Georgian buildings, mainly dating from the 18th century. Do explore this intriguing area which gives the appearance of being a village within a city.

19. **Canon Gate.** Having turned into South Street turn right passing under the 16th century gateway into Canon Lane. All the properties you see on this section of the walk are associated with the clergy.

20. **Palace Gate.** A 14th century gate house, positioned at the end of Canon Lane leads to the Bishop's Palace, which unfortunately cannot be visited. The Palace, a mellow brick and flint construction has been added to and remodelled over the last seven hundred years and therefore contains something of each era, beginning with the 13th century. The original Palace was destroyed by fire in 1187.

21. **Palace Gardens.** A walkway from Palace Gate will take you into the Palace Gardens. The walled garden is sheltered and filled with colourful annuals and perennials. Adjoining it is a lawned area planted with shrubs and trees.

22. **St. Richard's Walk.** Narrow and extremely picturesque, this flagged path leads into the cloisters. It's named after St. Richard, a Bishop of Chichester.

*Chichester Cathedral*

23. **The Bell Tower.** A separate Bell Tower was built for the Cathedral in the 15th century. It now houses the Cathedral Gift Shop on the ground floor.

24. **The Cathedral.** A masterpiece of Norman architecture that replaced its lesser predecessor at Selsey in 1075 as the centre of Christianity in Sussex. Having been damaged by fire in 1114 and again in 1187, the completed cathedral subsequently became the centre for thousands of pilgrims visiting the shrine of St. Richard, a Bishop of Chichester, who was canonized in 1262. The shrine was destroyed by Henry VIII in 1538. For the visitor today, there are informative leaflets and guides just inside the Cathedral entrance. These will give a detailed explanation of its history, the interior and great works of art.

*St Richard's Walk, Chichester*

*The Guildhall, Priory Park, Chichester*

# TOUR 16 - FARMS AND FARM SHOPS

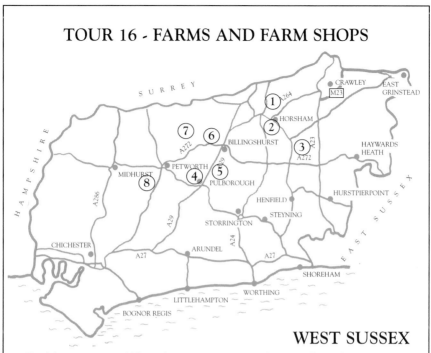

## WEST SUSSEX

1. Wattlehurst Farm, Kingsfold, Horsham
2. Horsham Museum, The Causeway, Horsham
3. Old Mill Farm Shop, Bolney
4. Brinsbury College, nr Pulborough
5. Acorn Shop, nr Pulborough
6. Fishers Farm Park, Wisborough Green
7. Kirford Growers Country Shop, Kirdford
8. Noah's Farmyard, Grittenham Farm, Petworth

*"Smile Please"*

# TOUR 16 - FARMS AND FARM SHOPS

*D'you remember the days when every farm had a picture postcard farmyard with hens and ducks pecking the dusty ground for corn. The nearby fields would have lambs playing amongst the remains of a hay stack whilst cattle munched contentedly on unfertilized grass. One could buy fresh eggs, with feathers attached, from the farmer's wife, together with a jug of milk, still warm from doe-eyed Daisy. A basket would be filled with misshapen potatoes, sweet crunchy carrots bearing their wilting headgear and crisp, earthy lettuces. Not that long ago 'harvest time' appeared to involve the entire village, finishing with the beery festivities of a harvest supper. Ploughing was done by a couple of huge Shire horses pulling an ancient plough and followed by a flock of seagulls.*

*But enough nostalgia; bring the kids and let's go in search of those farms today and see what we can find ....*

## WATTLEHURST FARM, KINSFOLD. HORSHAM (1)

Wattlehurst farm is located on the A24, five miles north of Horsham on the Surrey/Sussex border. It is not an enormous farm, but it's well laid out with spacious enclosures or barns for the animals, some of which are very unusual. A Llama called Solo, who is apparently rather shy, gazed at me from a great height as I wandered past to look at a couple of Emus sporting their curious gait and looking like relics from TV's 'Ministry of Silly Walks'. Enchanting wallabies, pygmy goats, pot bellied pigs and fallow deer are in paddocks side by side with Molly, the donkey, Lady the shire horse and Lottie the friendly sheep, not to mention all the various breeds of cattle and Pugwash, the Peruvian pig boar.

There is an admission charge to the farm, which is only open to the public on Sundays or Bank Holiday Mondays. However, special visits can be arranged from Monday to Friday and educational packs are available. For further information, telephone (01306) 627490.

## HORSHAM MUSEUM, THE CAUSEWAY. HORSHAM (2)

The one time market town of Horsham is historically best seen in the Causeway, where architecture, dating from the 16th century onwards has been beautifully preserved. At the top end is the 19th century Town Hall. It stands on the former site of a covered Market Hall and is adjacent to the tiny Market Square and the jettied Causeway House, home to Horsham Museum. Without doubt this has to be one of the best museums in Sussex; it contains a wealth of extremely well presented local information and has a free admission; so don't miss it. To the rear of the museum are attractive gardens, a range of outbuildings and a large 18th century Sussex barn. This is entirely devoted to the history of the Wealden farmer and gives an insight into farming throughout the centuries with displays of artifacts from the days of our great grandparents. How times have changes!

## OLD MILL FARM SHOP, BOLNEY (3)

Old Mill Farm Shop is signed from the A272, a short distance west of the A23 at Bolney. Both the farm and the shop are at the end of a long lane in attractive rural surroundings and it's difficult to believe the London - Brighton road, with its quantity of traffic is nearby. The shop sells all kinds of home-grown produce including, jams, marmalades, chutneys and pickles. There is an admission charge to visit the animals on the farm itself where, more often than not, the resident peacock struts around the entrance waiting to welcome you. Old Mill Farm is open every day from 10.30 a.m. to 5.30 p.m.

## BRINSBURY COLLEGE, NEAR PULBOROUGH (4)

You'll find Brinsbury College of Agriculture and Horticulture on the A29 between Billingshurst and Pulborough. To visit the College, which has its own commercial farm, has to be by prior arrangement, so it's really only for those interested in doing some sort of course in farming. However, every June, Brinsbury holds an Open Day for the public to look over the College, the farm and all the other associated working units together with the conservation area and nature trail. There is the chance to buy some jolly good plants from their horticultural section and children are well catered for with general amusements and tractor and trailer rides around the farm. For further information about Brinsbury College, telephone (01798) 873832.

## ACORN SHOP, NEAR PULBOROUGH (5)

Opposite Brinsbury College is the Acorn, a kind of Farm Shop with a difference. It opened in 1991 to provide a retail outlet for produce that is grown or made by students with learning difficulties. The Acorn Project is run by the Aldingbourne Trust, a non-profit making charity in partnership with the West Sussex County Council Social Services.

The well kept shop always has a selection of seasonal fruits and vegetables, home made cakes and pies, jams, chutneys, plants and fresh flowers. Included in the 'veggie' display are oriental green vegetables, mostly used in salads; names like Choy Sun, Indian Spinach, Japanese Greens, Mustard Greens, Clay Tonia and Shungiku, didn't mean much to me but they tasted delicious with a slightly hot, aromatic flavour. The Acorn is open from Monday to Friday and some Saturdays during the season.

## FISHERS FARM PARK, WISBOROUGH GREEN (6)

A truly sophisticated farm attraction that offers everything a child could possibly wish to see in the way of farm animals. Even when they get bored with stroking their furry friends of varying sizes, there's still plenty for the children to do; like visit the gift shop or the adventure play area, complete with Noah's Ark, the play barns (presumably for wet weather), together with a colourful bouncy castle. Alternatively, you could go for a woodland walk, a pony ride, a tractor ride or try your hand at go-karting. You can watch the rabbits in Rabbit City, the ducks on the duck pond, or go and meet Caspari, one of the biggest horses in the world and Lady

*Gipsy Caravan at Fishers Farm Park*

May, one of the smallest. In the animal barns, events take place throughout the day, such as bottle feeding of lambs and goat kids, milking cows or grooming horses. And when you're finally exhausted, you can collapse in the Tea Barn or restaurant for farmhouse style fare.

Fishers Farm Park is open every day and carries an admission charge. It's situated down a lane off the A272 between Billingshurst and Wisborough Green.

## KIRDFORD GROWERS COUNTRY SHOP, KIRDFORD (7)

A picture book village renowned for its glorious apple orchards that dot the local Wealden countryside. The Kirdford Growers Country Shop, a substantial complex with plenty of parking, offers three different varieties of Kirdford apple juice as well as ciders and other apple related produce. There is always a range of good country fare on sale including farmhouse cheeses, freshly baked bread and, of course, sweet home-grown apples. The adjoining Russets Tea Room provides a peaceful spot for that home-made cake and tea-time cuppa. The shop is open daily and is situated on the north west side of Kirdford.

## NOAH'S FARMYARD, GRITTENHAM FARM, PETWORTH (8)

Set in idyllic countryside bordering the River Rother, this 150 acre working farm presents a 'hands-on' experience with most of the farm animals, from horses right down to guinea pigs. The farmyard really does reflect something of that bygone era with the cows 'a-mooing' in the byres and chickens, ducks, a noisy cockerel and geese wandering around. The nature trail is lovely and eventually leads to the river bank with a special picnic area. Noah's Farmyard is situated off the A272, west of Petworth. It's open daily from Easter until September with an entrance charge.

# TOUR 17 - COLLECTABLE ANTIQUES

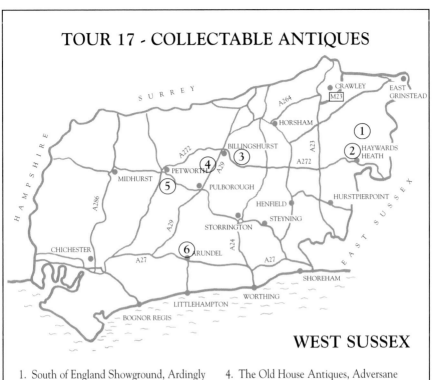

## WEST SUSSEX

1. South of England Showground, Ardingly
2. Lindfield
3. Billingshurst
4. The Old House Antiques, Adversane
5. Petworth
6. Arundel

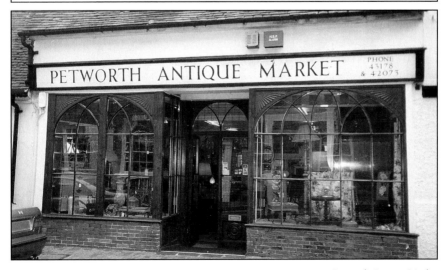

*Petworth Antique Market*

# TOUR 17 - COLLECTABLE ANTIQUES

*What could be more pleasurable than looking for that very special piece of furniture or bric-a-brac, combined with exploring a few of the historic towns and villages of West Sussex. This tour does just that. It travels more or less directly along the A272 after Ardingly and Lindfield, visiting Billingshurst, Adversane and Petworth, the antiques centre for the south. It then heads south to the attractive town of Arundel, dominated by the Duke of Norfolk's splendid castle, and overlooking the winding River Arun.*

*Ardingly and Billingshurst, however are 'occasional stops' only; for one holds Antique Fairs, the other, Auctions (see appropriate text). Should one of these happen to slot into your agenda, the rest of the tour would probably have to be pruned accordingly.*

## SOUTH OF ENGLAND SHOWGROUND, ARDINGLY (1)

Lying close to Ardingly on the B2028, is the South of England Showground, a major venue for various events including Antique Fairs. There are usually six two-day Antique Fairs a year; the first day for trade, the second for the public. Visiting one of these would take up half a day, possibly more, so you'd have to pick and choose what else, if anything, there would be time to do. Occasionally, there are much smaller one day Antique Fairs and these are usually held on a Sunday. For dates and further information, contact the Tourist Information Centre in Horsham on (01403) 211661.

## LINDFIELD (2)

A picturesque village with all the necessary ingredients for whiling away an enjoyable hour, whilst searching amongst the antique shops and markets for whatever takes your fancy. The long sloping village street is lined with Georgian and Queen Anne houses, interspersed with a few Tudor gems. At the top end of the

*The Corner Gallery, Lindfield*

High Street is the over restored but still handsome, Church of St. John the Baptist. At the bottom end lies the village green and pond, complete with ducks. It therefore seems incongruous that the urban tentacles of Haywards Heath surround this architectural pearl of a classically English village.

The antique shops start about half way up the main street and offer the expensive traditional pieces to a wide assortment of bric-a-brac. The Corner Gallery is particularly good for bargain hunting; this two floor antiques market appears to deal mainly in small items from any era, all displayed in tempting confusion. Two further centres, one more geared to furniture, are sited almost opposite. Most are open six days a week. For those collectors who are interested in radios and the like, there is a Wireless Museum, open on Tuesdays, Thursdays, Fridays and the first and third Saturdays of each month, a.m. only. There are two or three pubs (if not more) and at least one coffee shop all ready to supply much needed refreshments. Linfield lies slightly north of Haywards Heath on the B2112.

## BILLINGSHURST (3)

Sotheby's of Bond Street have their regional salerooms housed in the old Convent buildings at Summers Place, a little north of Billingshurst on the A29. They hold ongoing specialist and non-specialist auctions: so, before passing through this village with Roman origins (see Roman Sussex), telephone Sotheby's on (01403) 783933 to find out what's on their auction calendar. It could be just for you.

## THE OLD HOUSE ANTIQUES, ADVERSANE (4)

Do make a short detour from the A272 at Billingshurst and follow the A29 southwards, to Adversane. Sited right by the crossroads of the A29 and the B2133 at Adversane, is Old House Antiques; being set well back from the road means there is ample parking on the forecourt. This large, rambling property has, to my knowledge,

*The Old House Antiques, Adversane*

been trading in antiques for more than twenty years and has two uneven floors filled with furniture and curios, spilling from every corner. Amongst this chaotic, but enjoyable setting, The Old House serves coffee, light lunches and teas. To one side of the building is an over-sized shed, rather grandly called The Old Orchard Antiques Market. Here, the same atmosphere of disorder reigns, which makes searching through the bric-a-brac quite a task. The Old House is open daily, including Sundays.

## PETWORTH (5)

The lovely and ancient town of Petworth has slowly been suffocated by traffic congestion; the plans for the much needed by-pass remain, for one reason or another, elusively out of reach. So, instead of being able to wander leisurely around the shops and historical buildings (of which there are many), one must keep half an eye on the traffic, passing along the streets meant only for a horse and cart.

Since medieval times Petworth has been a prosperous and busy market town. It is still like that today, although the trades, of course, have changed. Known as the Antiques Centre for the South, there are more than fifteen antique shops and one antiques market, all sited 'twixt the church and the vicinity of the market square'. Take note though; you are unlikely to find junk or bargains in Petworth. It is truly the centre for fine furniture, porcelain, clocks or whatever the dealer happens to specialize in. It makes a very welcome change to see so many genuine pieces in a trade that is littered with fakes.

When you reach Petworth make for the car park; it's much easier than trying to park elsewhere and it's only a minute or two from the centre. The Tourist Information Centre by Market Square has a leaflet on all the antique shops and where to find them. Most are open from Monday to Saturday inclusive. If there's still a bit of time to spare, why not visit Petworth House, whose renowned art collection rivals that of many London galleries. Included in the exhibits are paintings by Titian, Turner, Gainsborough, Van Dyke and Reynolds. Petworth House and Park is owned by The National Trust and there is an admission charge to visit.

## ARUNDEL (6)

The final port of call on this tour is Arundel, four miles north of Littlehampton and sited by the Arun river. This picturesque hilltop town is dominated by the great Arundel Castle, of whose Norman remains are few (see Norman Sussex for further information). However, the castellated towers and spires of the Gothic reconstruction, soar into the sky like something from a childhood fairytale. There is much to see and do in Arundel and a quick visit to the Tourist Information Centre in the High Street, to pick up local leaflets, could be beneficial. All the antiques establishments, including picture galleries, are sited in the High Street and Tarrant Street, the main shopping thoroughfare between the Castle and the river, so you can't possibly miss them.

The antiques on sale are extremely varied and range from 18th century oak dressers to 20th century china egg cups and everything else in between: but beware, lurking amongst the real thing is quite a bit of reproduction, especially in some of the antiques centres.

# TOUR 18 - CRAFTS AND CRAFTSMEN

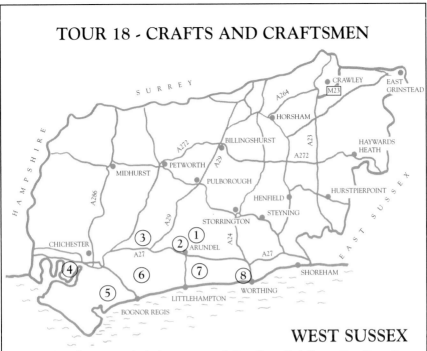

## WEST SUSSEX

1. Amberley Village Pottery, Amberley
2. Arundel
3. Slindon Pottery, Slindon
4. Bosham Walk Craft Centre, Bosham

5. Rose Green Craft Centre, Rose Green, Bognor
6. The Pottery, Shripney Lane, Shripney
7. Wood Design, Dappers Lane, Angmering
8. Bruun Farmelo Workshop, Worthing

*Bosham Walk Craft Centre, Bosham*

# TOUR 18 - CRAFTS AND CRAFTSMEN

*Today, the word 'Craft' has rather lost its true meaning. So often it's simply a disappointing array of baskets filled with mass produced gifts, bearing no resemblance whatsoever to individual pieces executed by an expert.*

*So what has happened to the craftsmen whose skills have sometimes been passed from generation to generation over hundreds of years? Villages, once the oyster of such traders, have now become residential and the main thoroughfare of any town is an expensive place to conduct a business. Out of necessity, the craftsman's venues for working and selling have had to change and sometimes it's not such an easy task to find them.*

*Tour 18 spends the day meandering through the country lanes to discover the potteries: into the seaside town of Worthing for hand painted silks and luxurious knitwear: a tiny industrial area in Angmering provides an unlikely setting for beautiful hand made furniture: then there's the Craft Centres where one can watch the craftsmen at work and see a wide range of their goods on sale. A few of the artisans mentioned are members of The Guild of Sussex Craftsmen and details of the Guild's special events held throughout Sussex can be obtained from Tourist Information Centres.*

## AMBERLEY VILLAGE POTTERY, AMBERLEY (1)

In the heart of this traditional and desirable village, there's an intriguing pottery whose premises are in the former Congregational Chapel. Like an Aladdin's cave, it's filled with rustic garden pots, crocks, bowls, mugs, jugs, platters, plates and the like, all handmade in the accustomed way. The wares are the work of several potters, all sharing the same exciting but chaotic workshop. This is in the main part of the chapel and to gain entry into the showroom behind, one has to pass by the kilns, chaos and potters: which is good really, because you get the chance to see their work in various stages of completion.

By contrast the showroom is beautifully laid out with dried flowers enhancing interesting pottery, glazed in the richest hues imaginable. It's not expensive either, so this makes Amberley a must if you're pottery hunting. And even if you're not, Amberley's lanes of enviable thatched cottages and pretty gardens beg to be explored. There's a good pub, a village shop, a 13th century church and even a castle of sorts (see Norman Sussex). The pottery is open daily and the telephone number is (01798) 831876. Amberley can be found to the north of the B2139, four miles west of Storrington.

*Amberley Village Pottery, Amberley*

# ARUNDEL (2)

Built on the slopes below Arundel Castle (see Norman Sussex), this ancient town offers a historic gem for the visitor. There are gift shops, restaurants and a surfeit of antique shops (see Collectible Antiques), but interspersed between this selection are one or two Craft Shops that are just a bit special.

Situated by the Tourist Information Centre in the High Street is Arundel Brass Rubbing Centre. Here, all the paper, waxes and a fine selection of brasses are supplied, so you can learn to make your own picture at leisure. Tarrant Street contains a shop called 'Needle Art', which specializes in fine tapestries and handicrafts; nearby is the Glass Studio, where you can observe the engraver at work and browse amongst unusual glassware. The Walking Stick shop is also in Tarrant Street and has hundreds and hundreds (and I'm not exaggerating) of handmade and antique walking sticks for sale.

Probably the most important thing about crafts in Arundel is the Art and Craft Festival, which takes place every year during August and lasts for three weeks. It's held at the Norfolk Centre by the lower entrance to the Castle and has in the region of a hundred exhibitors. Over sixty varieties of Arts and Crafts are shown with many of the participants demonstrating their skills and answering questions. You can even have a go at some of the crafts yourself.

## SLINDON POTTERY, SLINDON (3)

Slindon is an extremely attractive National Trust village, positioned on the downland just north of the A27/A29 junction between Arundel and Chichester. Slindon Pottery is at the top end of the village in the old Wheelwright's Shop. It's run by the accomplished Janet Upton, whose pottery is all handmade and mostly wheel-thrown in stoneware with a small range of earthenware. Her particular 'pieces de resistance' are stoneware clocks, either free standing or wall mounted with quartz battery movements. Most have some form of flora or fauna positioned above the hour. Established in Slindon since the 1970's, the workshop/showroom has a selection of other local crafts on sale and it's open daily except for Tuesdays. Telephone (01243) 814534.

## BOSHAM WALK CRAFT CENTRE, BOSHAM (4)

This first class craft centre is located in the quayside village of Bosham, whose attributes are covered in 'Canals, Creeks and Harbours'. Just a stone's throw from the estuary, a timbered property sports the hanging sign of a weather-beaten fisherman. This indicates Bosham Walk Craft Centre and you can't possibly miss it; just follow the aroma of coffee, for amongst all the craft stalls is a very pleasant coffee shop, The building itself has been sympathetically converted; the oak beams, flagged floors and generally unsophisticated appearance enhances both the artists' and the craftsmen's' work. Frequently, special exhibitions and demonstrations are held and these, together with the resident stalls of jewellery, pottery, dried flowers, hand- turned and carved wood, clock restoration, dolls houses, fretwork toys and an art gallery make Bosham an irresistible attraction. The Craft Centre is open daily and one can park in the small car park opposite. Bosham is signed from the A259, three miles west of Chichester.

## ROSE GREEN CRAFT CENTRE, ROSE GREEN, BOGNOR (5)

An emporium of Arts and Crafts, situated in a quiet street on the northern perimeter of Bognor. The craft work, both ancient and modern in style, is all done by professional craftsmen and there is much evidence of 'copper foil' Tiffany type stained glass.

Should you be interested in learning something about a particular craft, then Rose Green is your place, for tuition is their forte and a wide variety of courses, which could last one day or several weeks, are held at the studio. The subject might be: painting in water colours, lace making, stained glass (copper foil), pottery, silk painting, patchwork and many more; just enquire within. Rose Green Craft Centre is open daily except for Sundays and the phone number is (01243) 262059. Rose Green lies to the west of the B2166.

## *THE POTTERY, SHRIPNEY LANE, SHRIPNEY (6)*

A 17th century thatched barn, that most would consider ripe for conversion, provides the potter, Hugh Watson with a palatial, if draughty, studio. Having had thirty years of experience, his time is now divided between teaching in Chichester and the studio. All his handmade pottery is very reasonably priced and visitors are always welcome to browse or simply watch the pots being made at the wheel. However, it is advisable to check the opening times first, by phoning (01243) 823339. Shripney is located on the A29 just north of Bognor.

*Shripney Pottery*

# WOOD DESIGN, DAPPERS LANE, ANGMERING (7)

Whilst the village of Angmering is charmingly immaculate, the surrounds of Wood Design workshops in Dapper Lane are rather untidy. It's somewhat of a surprise when a hefty door in an oversized shed leads into a workshop-cum-showroom, filled with beautiful contemporary furniture and the evocative smell of resin, wax and wood shavings.

Brendan J. Devitt Spooner (am uncertain what the J. stands for), creates miracles from one of nature's loveliest materials - wood. He specializes in designing and making individual pieces of furniture such as tables, chairs and bookcases etc., from the more common hard woods. These could be Oak, Ash, Walnut, Yew, Sycamore or Cherry, together with the lesser known types such as Laburnum, Apple or Almond. Some pieces of furniture were commissioned from the trees that blew down in the hurricane of '87. One of these, a corner cabinet, has been featured on the television. Wood Design is open on weekdays only and the phone number is (01903) 776010. Angmering lies midway between A259 and the A27, west of Worthing.

# BRUUN FARMELO WORKSHOP, WORTHING (8)

The combined talents of a Danish fashion designer specializing in knitwear, and an English textile designer, painting on silk must, without doubt, be a recipe for success.

Susanne Bruun uses natural fibres for her flowing designs of knitted jackets, tops and dresses. Panels of silk are occasionally combined into the knitwear, making the article of clothing particularly eye-catching. John Farmelo hand paints long lengths of silk which are then made into garments, including a selection of stunning evening jackets. He also produces a range of scarves, ties and cushions. Both work from their home in Worthing and hold an 'open house' weekend around November or December. Otherwise, they are regularly seen at local exhibitions and fairs. People are always welcome to ring at any time and make an appointment to see their constantly changing range of knitwear and silks. (01903) 216125.

# PICK AND MIX GEOGRAPHICAL INDEX

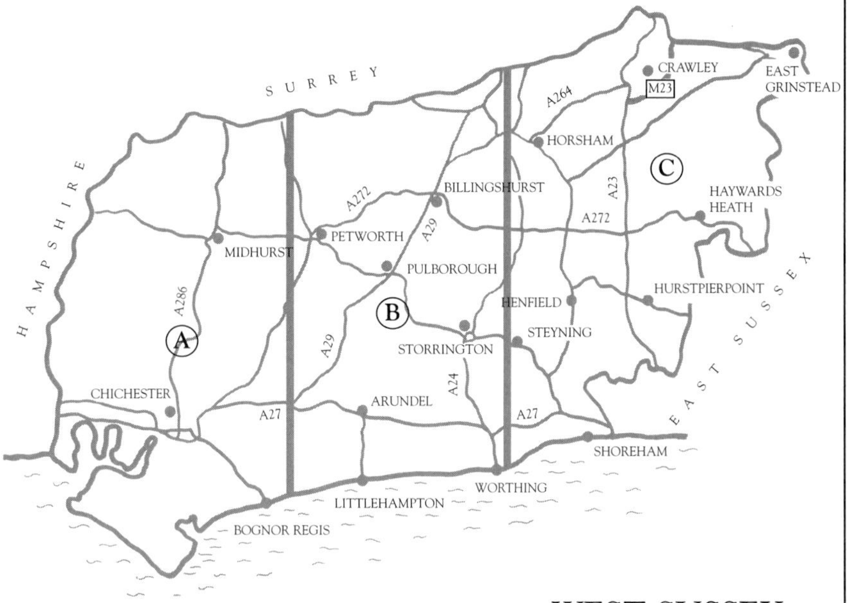

SURREY

CRAWLEY
M23
EAST GRINSTEAD

A264

HORSHAM

HAMPSHIRE

A272

BILLINGSHURST

A23

HAYWARDS HEATH

A272

MIDHURST

PETWORTH

A29

Ⓒ

A286

PULBOROUGH

HURSTPIERPOINT

Ⓐ

A29

STORRINGTON

Ⓑ

HENFIELD

STEYNING

EAST SUSSEX

CHICHESTER

A27

ARUNDEL

A24

A27

SHOREHAM

BOGNOR REGIS

LITTLEHAMPTON

WORTHING

## WEST SUSSEX

# A

# B

## C

*Floor mosaics, Bignor*

*Hypocaust, an underfloor heating system, Bignor*

# TOURIST INFORMATION CENTRES

**ARUNDEL**
61, High Street                                    Tel: (01903) 882268

**BOGNOR REGIS**
Belmont Street                                     Tel: (01243) 823140

**BRIGHTON**
10, Bartholomew Street                             Tel: (01273) 323775

**CHICHESTER**
29a, South Street                                  Tel: (01243) 775888

**FONTWELL**
Little Chef Complex                                Tel: (01243) 543269

**GATWICK**
Airport International Arrivals                     Tel: (01293) 560108

**HORSHAM**
9, The Causeway                                    Tel: (01403) 211661
                                                   (open Tues to Sat)

**HOVE**
Church Road                                        Tel: (01273) 778087

**LIITLEHAMPTON**
Windmill Complex,                                  Tel: (01903) 713480
Coastguard Road                                    (Summer only)

**MIDHURST**
North Street                                       Tel: (01730) 817322

**PETWORTH**
Market Square                                      Tel: (01798) 343523

**SHOREHAM**
Civic Centre                                       Tel: (01273) 455566

**WORTHING**
Chapel Road                                        Tel: (01903) 210022

*Boxgrove Priory*

**S. B. Publications** publish a wide range of local interest books about Sussex.
For a catalogue write (enclosing S.A.E.) to: S. B. Publications, c/o 19 Grove Road,
Seaford, East Sussex BN25 1TP